1 Hint Lanzarote ...in a different way!

By Andrea Müller

The content of this Book was compiled with the greatest care. Nevertheless, errors cannot be completely excluded. The author assumes no legal responsibility or any liability for any remaining errors and their consequences All trade names are used without guarantee of free usability and are possibly registered trademarks. All (also personal) images were explicitly permitted only for this travel guide. Any further use / transfer is expressly not permitted. The work including all its parts is protected by copyright. Any use - even in extracts - is only permitted with the author's consent. All rights reserved.

Comments and questions are welcome:

Andrea Müller

Calle Las Cuevas, 91 - A2

E- 35542 Punta Mujeres, Province of Las Palmas, Lanzarote

Web: www.lanzarote-mal-anders.de

mailto:ebook@lanzarote-mal-anders.de

© 2018 by Andrea Müller, Cover design: Andrea Müller

Number of pages Print variant: 84 pages

Number of images: 17 images / cards

2 Imprint (German)

Bibliographic Information of the German National Library

The German National Library lists this publication in the German National Bibliography; detailed bibliographic data are available on the Internet at http://dnb.d-nb.de

© 2020 Andrea Müller

Production and publishing
BoD - Books on Demand, Norderstedt

ISBN: 9783750480797

3   Introduction travel guide Lanzarote

Lanzarote is the second smallest of the eastern volcanic islands and impresses with 300 volcanoes, which are embedded in a uniquely fascinating, contrasting landscape.

The ever green, rugged and almost untouched north meets a fine sandy island centre, which changes into a volcanic moon and crater landscape with mountains of fire in the south.

To protect the natural beauty of the volcanic island and its cultural heritage, Lanzarote was declared a Biosphere Reserve by UNESCO on 07.10.1993.

Thanks to the significant island artist César Manrique, Lanzarote was nearly spared from the serious building sins that took place in the neighboured islands Tenerife and Gran Canaria in the years 1960-70. Take advantage of his unique commitment to discover the many small white villages and let yourself be impressed by his unique work.

La Graciosa [1] View of La Graciosa [2]

Haría [3] Arrieta and Punta Mujeres [4]

Jardín de Cactus [5] Teguise[6]

Fundación [7] Monumento al Campesino [8]

4 The short version from north to south

4.1 La Graciosa

The five islands Alegranza, Roque del Este, Roque del Oeste, Montaña Clara and La Graciosa belong to the Chinijo archipelago. **La Graciosa [1]** is separated from Lanzarote by the 1.2 km wide El Río inlet and is the only permanently inhabited island. Since October 2018 it is officially the eighth island of the Canary Islands archipelago.

The capital Caleta del Sebo, which is also the island's port, offers restaurants, shopping and accommodation. In the interior, the volcanoes Las Agujas with 266 m and Montaña del Mojón with 188 m rise. The Playa de las Conchas, that is located at the bottom of the Montaña Bermeja with 157 m, is considered as the most beautiful beach of the island. A ferry crosses regularly from the northernmost fishing village Órzola to La Graciosa in 30 minutes.

4.2 Mirador del Rio

The Mirador del Río viewpoint is located 475 m above the cliffs in a former military post. The building, designed by César Manrique, with its outdoor terraces and the view through the "eyes" offers a fantastic view of the island of **La Graciosa [2]**.

4.3 Haría

The municipality of **Haría [3] still** lives from agriculture. All around, potatoes, onions, peas and wine are grown. From the Mirador de Guinate you have a fantastic view of the coastal landscape and La Graciosa. From the Mirador de Haría viewpoint you can enjoy a fantastic view of the largest palm grove on the island, nicknamed the "Valley of a Thousand Palms". Every Saturday a large handicraft market is held in the centre of the village under old Indian laurel trees. Worth seeing is the last residence of the island artist, the Casa Museo César Manrique, the workshop of the last basket weaver on the island and the Taller municipal de Artesanía arts and crafts centre.

4.4 Arrieta and Punta Mujeres

The former fishing village **Arrieta [4]** on the east coast is characterized by whitewashed houses, as is the neighboring village **Punta Mujeres [4].** Next to the large bathing beach Playa de La Garita, the small natural swimming pools Piscinas Naturales invite you to swim. The Jameos del Agua cave is part of a 6 km long lava tunnel that runs from the La Corona volcano to the sea and continues under the sea floor for 1.5 km. Inside is a lagoon in which a white, blind crab, unique in the world, lives. In the same part of the tunnel is the accessible lava cave Cueva de los Verdes.

4.5   Guatiza

The small village of Guatiza was the centre of scale insect breeding on Lanzarote, where fig cacti were grown to produce the red pigment carmine. By returning to natural raw materials, the old cactus fields were reforested. In the Museum Museo de Cochinilla you will immerse yourself in history and become creatively involved in the new Asociación Milana.
Worth seeing is the cactus garden **Jardín de Cactus [5]** designed by César Manrique with more than 1400 cactus species.

4.6   Teguise

Teguise [6] was the island capital until 1852. Since the beginning of the year 2020, it has been one of the most beautiful villages in Spain and is nicknamed "La Villa" - the little town. In the center of the city you will find the parish church Iglesia Nuestra Señora de Guadalupe from where you will have a walk through the old town. The main attraction is the Sunday market Mercadillo de Teguise with over 500 stalls. Directly above the city, the former fortress Castillo Santa Barbara with a pirate museum is enthroned on the volcanic mountain. In the big holiday resort Costa Teguise you have the sandy beach Playa de las Cucharas and the small bay Playa del Jabillo. In the municipality of Nazareth, which belongs to the village, the former estate of the actor Omar Sharif, who was famous in the 1960s, is located in a volcanic rock. He became known as Doctor Zhivago and also as Lawrence of Arabia.
On the hill of Los Valles you will find the small Ermita de Las Nieves from where you have a fantastic view over the island up to Fuerteventura. In Famara, kitesurfers and surfers get their money's worth on the over 4 km of sandy beach.

4.7   Tahíche

Tahíche is a small suburb above the island capital Arrecife. The **Fundación César Manrique is** located in the district of Taro de Tahíche **[7]**. This house has underground lava bubbles and is one of the absolute highlights of Lanzarote.

4.8 San Bartolomé

San Bartolomé is located between the villages of Tías and Uga, on the edge of the main agricultural area of La Geria, which has the largest wine production area on the island.

In the geographical centre of the island there is a replica of a picturesque old farm village, the Casa Museo del Campesino with the high fertility statue **Monumento al Campesino [8]**, dedicated to the island's farmers.

The agricultural museum El Patio in Tiagua shows different types of mills as well as field and handicraft equipment.

In the ethnological museum Museo Etnografico Tanit, a collection of objects that were collected in the course of nearly 100 years in the island is exhibited.

4.9 Arrecife

The capital and port city of Arrecife is the seat of the Island Council and was home to the largest fishing fleet in the Canary Islands.

The former eyesore of Arrecife, a 17-storey high-rise building was converted into the Grand Hotel Arrecife and is the most distinctive point of the island. From the café on the **17th floor [1]** you have a wonderful view over the city to Puerto del Carmen and Fuerteventura. In front of the hotel is the city beach Playa de Reducto, which is a feast for the eyes at high tide.

A landmark of the city is the spherical bridge that connects the city centre with the fortress Castillo San Gabriel. The large cannons in front of the entrance come from the former military post of the Mirador del Río. From here, the long shopping street Calle León y Castillo invites to go shopping and to visit the Casa Amarilla with its insular temporary exhibitions.

Worth seeing is the church San Ginés with the figures of the city patron and the Madonna of the Rosary. At the adjoining picturesque Charco de San Ginés you can look from the small restaurants to countless fishermen's boats.

On the northern outskirts of the city, the fortress Castillo San José with drawbridge and moat was converted into the Museum of Contemporary Art Museo Internacional de Arte Contemporaneo MIAC under the direction of César Manrique. Not far from there is the harbour Puerto de los Mármoles, where the big cruise ships anchor.

4.10 Puerto del Carmen

The former port of **Puerto del Carmen [2]** is Lanzarote's largest holiday area with the long beaches of Playa de Matagorda, Playa de los Pocillos, Playa Grande and the beautiful views of Fuerteventura. An endless shopping mile runs through the centre with countless shopping facilities, pubs and restaurants.

4.11 Puerto Calero

The chic little marina **Puerto Calero[3]** offers a selection of restaurants and boutiques. From here the catamaran starts to the Papagayo beaches and the submarine to dive into the Atlantic Ocean.

4.12 Montañas del Fuego

The **national park Timanfaya [4]** in the fire mountains Montañas del Fuego is the main attraction of Lanzarote. At Islote de Hilario, in front of the restaurant El Diabolo, the access road of the 50 sq km large volcanic landscape ends. The area is located above a magma chamber, whose temperatures reach over 600 degrees Celsius already 10 m below ground. A breathtaking drive through the volcanic landscape and impressive demonstrations follow. Not far from the entrance to Timanfaya, at Echadero de Camellos, there is the possibility of a dromedary ride on the slope of the volcano.

The **Centro de Visitantes [5]** offers an exhibition and film screenings on the subject of volcanoes. There are also free guided hikes, such as the Tremesana hike through the National Park. In Mancha Blanca is the sanctuary of the Ermita de Nuestra Señora de los Dolores, dedicated to the patron saint of the island.

4.13 Yaiza

The small town of **Yaiza [6], which has** won first place in beauty contests several times, is the centre of the district of the same name. On Corpus Christi large colourful salt carpets are strewn on the forecourt of the church, and during the Advent season a miniature replica of the island is erected.

There are 3 other attractions in the coastal area: the Salinas de Janubio, the natural spectacle of Los Hervideros and the fishing village of El Golfo.

4.14 Femés

The small village of **Femés [7]** is located on the edge of the natural protected mountain massif Los Ajaches and is the shortest connection to Playa Blanca. At an altitude of 350 m the forecourt of the church offers an indescribable view over Playa Blanca to Fuerteventura.

4.15 Playa Blanca

Only since the middle of the 1980s has the tiny fishing village Playa Blanca developed into the third largest holiday area on the island. Besides the artificially created main beaches Playa Flamingo and Playa Dorada, the **Papagayo beaches [8]** with their 7 different sized bays are the "non plus ultra".

In the harbour of Playa Blanca the ferries to Fuerteventura leave every hour. The snow-white dune landscape and the beaches in Corralejo are among the highlights of the neighbouring island.

5   The visitor centres- Centros de Arte, Cultura y Turismo

You can visit 9 centres, of which 8 are fee-based and up to 6 can be purchased at a reduced price as a combination bonus ticket.

In the north of the island, on the top of the Risco de Famara, is the viewpoint **Mirador del Río [1]**, from which you have a fantastic view of the offshore island of **La Graciosa [2]**. The cave **Cueva de los Verdes [3]** leads you through a long lava tunnel, exploring the **heart of the earth [4]**. In the **Jameos del Agua [5]** you can observe the unique small crabs in a cave and take beautiful photos in front of a brilliant **bathing area [6]** and in the cactus garden **Jardín de Cactus [7]** with the picturesque windmill you can see more than **1400 species of cacti [8]**.

The free Casa Monumento al Campesino, with the farmer's museum house and the fertility statue, is located in the geographical centre of Lanzarote, from which access is possible to any point on the island.

Near Arrecife, in the old military fortress of Castillo San José, you will find the International Museum of Contemporary Art (MIAC) with modern works of art, while to the south, in the Timanfaya National Park, are the Fire Mountains (Montañas del Fuego), created by volcanic eruptions between 1730 and 1736.

Different combination tickets, so-called BONO tickets, are offered with which you can save up to 10.55 €. They are valid for 14 days. Children up to 6 years are free, from 7- 12 years half price is charged.

Bono 3 centres: 21€🍾. You can choose from Jameos del Agua, Montañas del Fuego and the Cueva de los Verdes, 2 centres. Then you have to choose between the Mirador del Río and the Jardín del Cactus.

Bono 4 centres: 28€🍾. Here are the Jameos del Agua, the Cueva de los Verdes and the Montañas del Fuego. As the fourth centre you

can again choose between the Mirador del Río and the Jardín del Cactus. Maximum saving 6,80 €.
Bono 6 centres: 33€ ♦. With this ticket all centres can be visited.
Visiting hours: (Summer: 1 July - 30 September)
Jardín del Cactus: ☉summer 9am - 5.45pm, winter 10am - 5.45pm
Mirador del Río: ☉Summer 10 - 18.45, Winter 10 - 17.45
Montañas del Fuego: ☉Summer 9- 18.45, last trip: 18.00, Winter 9-17.45, last trip 17.00
Museo Internacional de Arte MIAC: ☉all year round,10- 20
Monumento al Campesino: ☉all year round,10- 17.45
Cueva de los Verdes: ☉all year round 10-19 h, last visit 18 h
Jameos of Agua: ☉all year round, 10 - 18.30
BONO tickets are available on request at all ticket offices in the centres. Not combinable with the Bono ticket are the Casa Amarilla in Arrecife with temporary, insular exhibitions and the underwater museum Museo Atlántico, for which a diving licence is required.

5.1   Mirador del Rio

In the extreme north, the **Mirador del Río [1]** at 475 m is the highest viewpoint in Lanzarote, offering a magnificent view of the cliffs of the Famara Mountains and the island of La Graciosa. The building designed by the island artist César Manrique was finished in the year 1973 and captivates by its volcanic stone front that adapts to the environment like a camellion and is therefore not obviously noticed. The wrought-iron steel sculpture, a combination of fish and bird, decorates the entrance to the Mirador.
A winding tunnel leads into two large vaults, in front of which are the large window facades, the so-called "eyes" of the viewpoint.
You can access the magnificent viewing platform, which juts out into the deep abyss, through the side doors of the cafeteria. Here, the robust railing gives you the feeling of standing at a ship's railing and soon you will be approaching the picturesque neighbouring island La Graciosa.
At the back of the cafeteria, the dynamically curved spiral staircase leads to the upper floors of the mirador with a souvenir shop, a seating area with a view of Monte Corona, the highest volcano in the north, and another viewing platform, from which you can again see **La Graciosa [2].**
On clear days the view from the Mirador is a feast for the eyes, but on cloudy days, apart from low clouds, you can see absolutely nothing. In these cases only the architecture of the viewpoint can be admired.

To enjoy the almost identical view of La Graciosa, park your rental car at the Mirador del Río and walk along the small street on the left side before the viewpoint. Alternatively, turn left into this street and pass the coast. There are small parking bays and wall openings on the land side where you can park your car.

Nostalgia: For the 1979 Christmas series on ZDF "Tim Thaler, the laughter sold", the shooting took place in the Mirador del Río, the Baron's residence, among other places.☻ daily summer 10-18.45 hrs- winter 10-17.45 hrs ⌂ signposted, LZ- 203- Carretera de Yé- 35541 Haria

5.2   Las Cuevas de Los Verdes

The cave system Las **Cuevas de Los Verdes [4] is** located in the north of the island and is integrated into the wide volcanic landscape of Malpais de la Corona. When the volcano La Corona erupted more than 3000 years ago, a 6 km long underground volcanic tunnel was formed, which extends from the volcanic cone to the sea. In this tunnel are the Cuevas de los Verdes and further down, just before the sea, the Jameos del Agua.

A visit to the cave is a journey into the flaming, cooled heart of the earth, spectacular and unique at the same time.

An area of about 1 kilometre in length can be visited. It consists of overlapping galleries with vertical connections that allow levels to be seen from different perspectives. You can see lava channels, as well as solid blocks carried away by the lava flow, lava drops, saline deposits and solidified lava layers. The vault and walls appear in spectacular colours **[4]**.

The tour of the interior of the earth takes about 50 minutes. After you have purchased the ticket, groups of about 50 people are grouped together. After a short briefing in Spanish and English, we quickly make our way through the cave from a mix of up and down stairs, back to normal straight ahead, sometimes even bent.

Inside there is a constant temperature of 20 degrees. At points of particular interest, the guide will give brief explanations. Shortly before the end of the tour it gets really exciting and fascinating. The guide points to a fabulously deep hole in the cave with the announcement: "No Pictures, no Pictures, children please stay behind, take care", as the barrier consists of a parapet that is not even knee-high. You will learn everything else on site.

① Make sure you wear sturdy shoes, flip-flops are not suitable. There are no toilets in the whole complex. You will find the next locations in front of the Cuevas de los Verdes on the side of the parking lot.

background information: The internal construction of the caves began in the 1960s and was completed in 1964. The lighting was setup by Jésus Soto, one of César Manrique's closest collaborators. Among other things, he also realized the Lagomar and determined the volcano route through the Timanfaya area.

Worth knowing: Las Cuevas de los Verdes means translated the "Caves of the Green". However, they are not called so because they are located in the green north of the island, but because the Verde family, translated as "green", lived here at that time.

When Lanzarote suffered from pirate attacks in the 16th and 17th centuries, the tangled galleries of the cave served as a hiding place and refuge for the island's inhabitants. ☉daily 10-19, last visit 18 h ⌂ signposted, LZ-1> LZ-204- 35542 Arrieta

5.3 Jameos del Agua

The cave system **Jameos del Agua [5]** is located in the north, on the LZ-1 towards Orzola and was formed by the eruptions of the volcano La Corona. The word Jameos comes from the vocabulary of the indigenous people, the Guanches, and means opening or deepening in the ground. The overall concept of the complex was designed by César Manrique and opened in 1966.

After the entrance a curved lava stone staircase leads down to the first level of the jameo, which ends in a restaurant. In the rear part there is a bar area harmoniously set into the cave walls, next to which the illuminated tunnel, which comes directly from the La Corona volcano, has been set in scene.

Past lush green plants, the next curved staircase leads directly to the lake with the crabs.

It is a small white, blind crayfish, which otherwise only occurs at depths of over 2,000 metres and grows to a maximum of 1.5 cm.

The water level of the lake sinks and rises with the tides, as the grotto is fed by seawater seeping through the rock, despite the lack of connection to the sea.

A narrow lava stone path to the back of the jameo. Although the lake appears deep, it is shallow because the high ceiling is impressively reflected on the water surface.

About in the middle of the lake you can see an opening in the vaulted ceiling through which daylight enters. This was caused by an explosion when the lava came into contact with the sea water, so that the penetrating light rays were reflected on the water surface.

When you arrive at the back of the lake, you will see the fascinating reflections of the entrance side on the water surface. Once again, seats invite you to linger. Stairs lead sideways to the next level with a bar and seating. It is fascinating from how many different levels the light reflections in the lake and the thick lava rock can be perceived. Further stairs lead to the next level to the outside area, where stairs also open up a small green garden landscape. The second fascinating attraction of the complex is located outside: a shrill, alpine white pool landscape with turquoise blue water, interspersed with black monoliths. It forms an extreme contrast to the dark boulders and transforms the place into an oasis, which invites to a photo shoot. The diagonally high palm tree is reflected in the pool and makes all pictures a perfect photo motif **[6]**.

Downstairs on the left side, the unusual bar creation with thick black lava stones, which serve as seats for the bar stools, catches the eye.

To the left of the pool, the path leads to the auditorium with 600 seats in 19 ascending rows. It is located in an impressive volcanic tunnel, where regular events take place again after repairs.

Outside, a spiral staircase again leads to the starting level. From two large terraces with a bar you can enjoy a fantastic view over the whole pool complex, the sea and the Malpais de La Corona.

From the right terrace you can reach the volcanic house Casa de los Volcanes, which is being renovated since mid-2019. At present the tour ends in the souvenir shop of the complex.☉ daily 10-18.30 h, ⌂ signposted, LZ-1> LZ-204, Carretera S/N- 35542 Arrieta

5.4   *Jardín de Cactus*

The cactus garden **Jardín de Cactus [7]** is located on the road between Guatiza and Mala. Already from the distance you can see a small windmill with a red roof, which serves as a signpost.

In front of the entrance the oversized, 8 m high green steel cactus is enthroned. The symbol of the complex was designed by the island artist César Manrique.

In the past, cochineal plants were grown on prickly pears throughout the area between Guatiza and Mala. Originally they come from Mexico and produce a carmine that has been used since the Aztecs for dyeing fabrics, food and cosmetics. In the year 1835 they arrived in Lanzarote. Offshoots of the cacti were planted in the spring and, if sufficiently large, infected with insects. In summer they were carefully harvested with tin spoons. The process of drying and cleaning to preserve the cochineal as a whole was meticulous and strictly traditional. However, since the red dye was artificially produced, breeding lost importance. At the moment, due to the return to natural raw materials, cochineal breeding has experienced a revival.

César Manrique took advantage of an abandoned volcanic pit to realize his idea of a large cactus garden. More than 10,000 plants can be admired, of which more than 1,000 belong to cactus species and thick leafed plants. The garden has the shape of an amphitheatre with terraces [8]. In the middle of the complex, the flower beds are larger and decorated with huge monoliths. In the rear part, next to a souvenir shop, there is a snack bar, where you can relax with a drink and feel the whole atmosphere again. ☼daily summer 10-18.45 h- winter 10-17.45 h, ⌂ signposted, LZ- 1>LZ-1A - Avenida Garafia- 35544 Haria

5.5   *Casa- Museo César Manrique*

The **Casa Museo César Manrique [1]** was the last residence of the important artist César Manrique. It is located in Haría and is indicated on all road signs in the town.

In 1987, the artist gave up his former home in Tahíche, the seat of today's Fundación César Manrique, and moved to his new house in Haría. He built it on the ruins of an old historic house that belonged to the village doctor Paco Fierro and lived there until his tragic accidental death.

The 12,000 square meter property is littered with massive old palm trees. The residential house is located in the right front part, the artist's large studio is located separately in the rear part of the grounds.

Small, black lava stones, which are spread all over the property, lead to the entrance. In the small inner courtyard, the so-called lemon courtyard, the cash desk is on the left side. There you will receive a map with additional information about the rooms of the house. Unfortunately no photos may be taken inside the house, only outdoor shots and photos in the studio are allowed. The tour begins on the right-hand side.

First you will enter the gallery courtyard, which was designed by Manrique with traditional old utensils. On the right-hand side on the upper floor there is a picturesque, traditionally made wooden lattice balcony. When you enter the building, you are standing directly in the dressing room for guests with an adjacent bathroom. Afterwards you will reach the hallway from the inner courtyard of the house. The heavy, dark wooden ceiling and the terracotta floor decorated with stars are reminiscent of the traditional architecture of the island. On the left side you will find a bedroom and bathroom. Due to the original arrangement of the artist's utensils, there is a constant feeling that César Manrique could walk back in at any moment. In the spacious bathroom, the interior and exterior form a harmonious unit through a light glass porch. Countless cosmetic items on the shelf above the washbasin completed the overall picture.

Back through the bedroom, past the hallway, you enter the living room, the largest and most central room of the house. A small bathroom, a kitchen and a dining room are attached here.

The small interior bathroom appears as bright as day due to the surrounding mirrors and circular recesses in the ceiling.

The kitchen next door is in country house style. It has a hatch to the living room and has an exit to a covered pergola.

The open living room, with views to the outside, is dominated by a basalt fireplace decorated with clay pots. In front of it there is a comfortable seating area. Next to it, on the frame of an old sewing machine stand a filled liquor bar. A black wing with countless photographs completes the living room interior.

In the adjoining dining room, at the long dining table, the first meeting in which the foundation of the César Manrique Foundation was decided took place.

In the outdoor area in front of the pool, another bedroom and bathroom area adjoins the building.

Behind the pool there are two groups of seats and sunbeds, which are covered by a pergola.

Finally, there is the possibility to watch a film about the artist on a flat screen outside next to the dining room. You can also find the shown report on YouTube: Taro, El eco de César Manrique.

The further way leads to the **studio [2]**, which is located in the rear part of the property.

César Manrique retired here every day to work. The workshop is littered with tables full of drawings, easels, tins of acrylic varnish and all kinds of objects. Everything has been preserved as the artist left it before his death in 1992. ☉all year round 10.30-18.00, ⌂ signposted, Calle Elvira Sánchez, 30- 35544 Haria

5.6 *Castillo San José*

The International Museum of Contemporary Art (Museo Internacional de Arte Contemporáneo MIAC) is located in the **Castillo San José [3]**, which served as a military fortress. It was built in the 18th century during the reign of the Bourbon Carlos III.

Thanks to the initiative of César Manrique, the dilapidated building was converted into a museum and opened in 1975. The artist personally supervised the reconstruction and development work, but hardly changed the inner structure of the castle. In the outbuildings, Manrique designed a restaurant, which is the most striking intervention in the architecture of the old fortress.

Payment is made in the container on the left side of the castle.

Access to the building is via the old drawbridge. Impressive are the thick vaulted walls where temporary art exhibitions are located.

Follow the stairs to the upper floor, looking from the industrial port of Muelle de Los Mármoles to the highest building in the city, where the Gran Hotel Arrecife is located.

The QUÉ MUAC restaurant is located in the basement, which can be reached via a curved staircase.

From the restaurant, one reaches the entrance area again by stairs upwards through another gallery.

① Even without a visit to the museum, you can reach the restaurant **QUÉ MUAC [4]** via the outside staircase that descends to the left of the museum. ☼All year round 10-20 hrs, ⌂ signposted, Carretera los Castillos- 35550 Arrecife

5.7   *Fundación César Manrique*

The **Fundación César Manrique [5]** was founded in 1982 by the island artist and a group of his closest friends and officially inaugurated in 1992. It is a private, cultural foundation that is financially self-sustaining, non-profit-making and promotes artistic activity in the natural and cultural environment.

The estate, with its farm buildings and garages, was personally transformed by César Manrique to be used as a museum within the framework of his foundation.

The complex is located on a 30.000 square metres big property that is crossed by deep black lava flows that were originated by strong volcanic eruptions in the years 1730 up to 1736.

The building was constructed on five large underground lava bubbles. The pure living space amounts to 1,800 square meters, to which 1,200 square meters of terraces and gardens still belong.

The upper floor is rather plain in the style of the traditional architecture of Lanzarote, but on closer inspection you will notice that Manrique has completely integrated nature into the house. The basement is pure fascination. Five large lava bubbles were connected by small cave passages through basalt tunnels and made habitable. In the green outdoor area there is a recreation area with pool, dance floor, sitting area and barbecue. In the last part of the house you will meet the artist's large studio.

Following a detailed description: The signposted Fundación is located at LZ-1 in Tahiche. Already on the parking lot there is a big white wind chime on the left side. It is called La Energía de la Pirámida, the energy of the pyramid. From here you can see the Gran Hotel Arrecife and the white dunes of Corralejo in Fuerteventura.

Continue through the entrance gate designed by Manrique to the pay house, which is on the left. You will pass a typical lava stone field with semi-circular lava walls like in the wine growing area of La Gería, follow a colourful wind chime on the right and an eroded sculpture, and arrive at the entrance of the house. On the entrance door, made of dark, solid wood, hangs a small doorplate in the form of a key with the inscription Manrique. Now you enter the small courtyard where you can see the upper openings of two lava bubbles on the right side. The branches of a palm tree protrude from one of these openings. On the walls hang white bones and objects that serve as decoration.

Continue to the left directly into the light-flooded living room with adjoining former kitchen, in which there is a small exhibition of pictures. Apart from the direct, fantastic view to the lava flows with the volcanoes behind them, the circular railings in the living room are immediately noticeable. Here there is a direct connection to the underlying volcanic bubbles. According to the story, the larger one, from which a tree rises, was the bubble that Manrique was the first to discover in the black lava field. On closer inspection he found that a **fig tree [6]** grew from a lava bubble.

From the balustrade behind it, a narrow spiral staircase, which unfortunately is not accessible, leads directly to the volcanic bubble, which is located under the living room.

Past a wall of mirrors, the tour first leads to the outside area. From here you can look over the black lava fields to the snow-white beaches of Fuerteventura.

On the way to the next showroom you will see the green pool area of the house on the lower left. Once inside the building, the room opens up a wide view of the fascinating lava landscape through its large window front.

Here you will find a documentation of the Lanzarote works of César Manrique: Mirador del Rio, Jameos del Agua, Restaurant El Diablo in the Timanfaya- National Park, Jardín de Cactus and Museo Internacional de Arte Contemporáneo. Furthermore, views of a draft of the cemetery portal with garden in Cadíz, a floor plan of the Mirador del Río and the Mirador El Palmarejo on La Gomera, and watercolour drawings are shown.

On the right side of the river is a table with its most important work: 1968- Jameos del Agua in Haría, 1968- Taro de Tahíche in Teguise, 1969- Casa del Campesino in San Bartolomé, 1970- Restaurante El Diabolo in the National Park Timanfaya, 1971- Complejo Costa Martíanez in Puerto de la Cruz auf Teneriffa, 1973- Mirador del Río in Haría, 1974- Castillo San José in Arrecife, 1977- Auditorio De Los Jameos Del Agua in Haría, 1982- La Vaguada in Madrid, 1989 Mirador de La Peña on the island of El Hierro, 1990- Jardín del Cactús in Teguise, 1991- Jardín de Palmajero in Valle Gran Rey auf La Gomera und 1992- Playa Jardín in Puerto de la Cruz on Teneriffa.

Through a hallway, with bright floors and walls, a lava basin embedded in the wall, above which there is a green fern, you enter the living room of the property.

There is a frontal fireplace made of lava stones and to the right of it the duster stairs leading down to the basement to the lava bubbles.

Two steps lead into the next rooms. In the first one, a wall-sized mirror on the left side immediately catches the eye. In two corners the tile mirror does not go through to the wall. Here, plants have been embedded in volcanic ash so that one has the feeling that the plants are growing out of the floor. Once again, the "green corners" are emphasized by ferns suspended from the ceiling.

The second room shows an exhibition of sketches, drawings, small sculptures and clay works by the artist.

To the right, you now reach the volcanic bubbles in the basement via a lava staircase planted on the sides.

In the first bubble you pass a small black pebble fountain and go through the first basalt passage into the second bubble. Here there is a white seating area set along the wall with a marble table and a palm tree.

It is fascinating that the palm tree protrudes from the open bubble. You will encounter a harmonious combination of different colours and lava layers.

In the next bubble, three red seating groups were arranged. Now you are directly under the living room. In the middle there is the tree that Manrique had seen on the lava field. At the back of the bubble the narrow spiral staircase leads up into the living room.

Passing a bathroom, we continue to the **inner courtyard [7]**, which is also of volcanic origin and is lushly planted with palm trees and cacti. There is a seating area hidden in the rock, a barbecue area and a small snow-white pool with turquoise blue water.

Now leave the green oasis through a **basalt passage [8]** and enter the fourth bubble, which is supported by 4 corner pillars. The passage leads down to the last bubble. Here again, a tree is arranged in the middle, with its tip protruding from the bladder opening. The seating groups and the lamps are chequered yellow and white. Again, plants with volcanic stones were embedded in the white soil.

From the last bubble, the route leads directly to Manrique's large, former studio, where a permanent exhibition of the artist's work is presented.

On the left side a large lava rock protrudes into the room, separated from the outside only by a gas disk.

You will have the feeling of standing directly in a lava field. In all other rooms a thick lava lump protrudes from one corner each.

On leaving the studio, you can see on the right side a bathroom almost hidden by plants. Upstairs, the public toilets are on the left-hand side.

The path continues into a large courtyard with a small black pond. In the middle the water splashes out of a lava rock. A long, large colourful mural by the artist adorns the left wall. Small volcanic stones were used for the outlines and pieces of tiles for the interior surfaces.

After this, there is a snack bar on the left side in the former garages, followed by a souvenir shop. The adjoining, roofed seating areas invite you to linger for a while.

☻ all year round 10- 18 h, ⌂ signposted, LZ-34- Calle Jorge Luis Borges,16- 35507 Tahiche

Space for personal notes...🖊...

5.8   *Lagomar- Casa Omar Sharif*

The former house of Omar Sharif, or as it is called today, the **Lagomar [1]** is located directly in and in front of a volcano, which is located above the village of Nazareth. Take the LZ-10 towards Teguise, turn off at the sign MUSEO and follow the road until you reach the "broken mountain".

On the slope of the volcano, in an old quarry, this unique **property [2]** was designed by César Manrique and realized by Jésus Soto in the 1970s. The artists created a fairy tale like from 1000 and one nights.

The legend: When the actor Omar Sharif visited the house during his shooting for the movie "Ruler of a Sunken World" he was so overwhelmed by its fascination that he decided to buy it immediately. However, after the infamous bridge game in which he lost the house, it fell into the hands of various owners. It is said that a real estate agent knew about Sharif's passionate bridge playing and asked him to play. Not knowing that his opponent was European champion, Sharif put his newly acquired house on the line in the belief that he would win the game. He lost and left his house, which he had owned for only one day, and never returned to Lanzarote. Since then the property has been known as Casa Omar Sharif.

In 1984 the German architect Dominik Böttinger travelled to the Canary Islands and when he arrived in Lanzarote he felt attracted by the magic of the house. After five years he was the new owner of the estate and returned to the island with his wife to tackle the last phase of the Lagomar.

Captivated by the uniqueness of this place, the couple decided to open it to the public. For this purpose, a restaurant was to be built in a part of the quarry. Their vision was to create a space that would delight all the senses and where art exhibitions, gastronomy and concerts would take place.

Once again, it was César Manriquewho advised the architect couple, so that the Lagomar could be opened in 1997.

ⓘ A visit to the estate is highly recommended and forms a symbiosis of all the objects worth seeing that Manrique and Soto have realised on the island. Another highlight is the white tubular tunnel through which you can walk on wooden steps over the water. As the property is situated in the quarry, you will enjoy a fantastic view of Arrecife, the highest building of the Grand Hotel. After the tour you will understand why Omar Sharif fell in love with the property.

✆ changeable- Google, ⌂ signposted, LZ-10> Calle los Loros,2-35539 Nazaret

5.9   *Castillo de Santa Bárbara - Museo de la Pirateria*

The Pirate Museum is located in the castle **Castillo de Santa Bárbara [3]** in Teguise. As soon as you approach the old island capital, you will discover the Castillo above the city on a volcanic mountain.

You drive up the winding road to the castle and can park your car right in front of the entrance. From there you can enjoy a wonderful **view over Teguise [4]**. On a clear day you can see Costa Teguise, Arrecife, Fuerteventura and the Fire Mountains as far as the island of Graciosa.

In order to protect the island population from pirate attacks at that time, a fortress was built in the 16th century on the remains of a small fort from the 14th century.

However, the fortress was so badly damaged by the siege of pirates that the Spanish crown ordered the reconstruction of the castle. After 10 years of construction the Castillo was completed in 1596. In 1991, after two years of renovation, the castle was turned into a museum.

Access is via a wide stone staircase with thick metal chains. A small drawbridge leads directly into the courtyard. The cash desk is on the left side. After payment you will receive a flyer with short information about the history.

The exhibition offers everything that could be collected here about pirates: Sailing ship models, including an 18th century warship with mini-cannons on board, an old ship's bell, a plumb bob, a sextant and, among other things, old revolvers.

Furthermore, colourful posters with brief information about the following pirates decorate the rooms: Francis Drake, Jean Fleury, Woodes Rogers, Walter Reigeigh, Morato Arráez, Le Clerc and Sores, George Clifford, Robert Blake, Tabac Arraez and Soliman. The information on the posters is only written in Spanish and English.

In the basement of the building, a film screening entitled "Nelson en Canarias" will take place, showing how Admiral Nelson wanted to conquer Santa Cruz in Tenerife. From the upper floor you again have a fantastic view over the whole island.

✆ changeable- Google, ⌂ signposted, LZ-10> Calle Herrera y Rojas,5- 35530 Teguise

5.10 The farm monument - Monumento al Campesino

The **Monumento al Campesino [5] is** located on the LZ-20 road in the municipality of San Bartolomé, in the geographical centre of the island, with access to all points of the island. Already from the distance you can see the big white sculpture, which is the landmark of this place. It stands on a lava stone hill, is only 15 metres high, but immediately catches the eye.

According to the design drawing by César Manrique, which can also be seen in the Fundación CM, the construction was realized in 1968 by his closest collaborator Jésus Soto. The sculpture, welded together from water tanks of old fishing boats, is called a fertility monument and depicts a farmer with his herd of goats.

Directly behind the monument is the **farming village [6]**. The complex is picturesquely white, small and well maintained. Follow the path to the right and you will come to the busy courtyard. In the 10 adjacent studios, the new sustainable market Mercado Autóctono sostenible, or MAS for short, takes place daily.

At the Agricultura Ecologica you can buy organic food and taste freshly squeezed juices or island wines. In the next workshop you can make aromatic salts and oils and buy soaps. In the bodega, island style is once again available for testing. In the Atelier Queso-Mermelada you will take part in a tasting of homemade jams, goat cheese and mojo sauces. In the Artesania de Cuero you can watch the production of leather goods and even buy sandals with goatskin. In the studio Mojo Rosetas you make Mojo sauces yourself and make your own bracelet or bookmark from natural raw materials. In the adjoining sombrería there is a large selection of handmade hats available. In the Ceramica you can watch Jochín making authentic Canarian ceramics or create your own clay souvenir with him. In the Atelier Tinte con Cochinilla you can buy textiles dyed with the natural Cochenille colour or buy the dye to take away. In the neighbouring room you will take part in a workshop on the processing of typical gofio flour. The centre's souvenir shop completes the shopping offer. ☉ Mon- Sa 10-17.45, depending on the artist also Sun, 15 July - 15 Sept 9-17.45, ⓦworkshops: Duration 20- 30 min., ♨3 € p.p.

The large spiral staircase in the middle of the farming village leads through a "black hole in the ground" to the lower part of the complex. The following lava entrance ends in a large restaurant, which is mainly used by organized bus tours for lunch. If you now go up the grand staircase, you will reach **the Café des Monumento al Campesino [7]**.

The beautiful ambience invites you to linger. The prices are reasonable, so that during the weekends one mainly finds islanders. Besides traditional dishes, the menu offers tapas typical of the island, a small selection of which is presented in the bar: marinated olives, pickled cheese and fish, marinated tuna cubes, stockfish, pulpo, marinated tomatoes, Russian salad and tomatoes stuffed with tuna salad.

✪ all year round 10- 17.45, ⌂ signposted, junction LZ-20+ LZ-30- 35559 Mozaga

5.11 Casa Amarilla - Arrecife

Casa Amarilla [8], the so-called yellow house, is located in Calle León y Castillo, at the beginning of the main shopping street in Arrecife.

The building was the former seat of the island government. It was built in the 1920s, declared a cultural asset of special interest in 2002 and extensively renovated in 2014. Temporally changing presentations that reflect the island's history take place in the exhibition rooms. ① Current exhibition at: www.cactlanzarote.com ✪change- Google, ⌂ Calle Léon y Castillo, 6- 35550 Arrecife

6   La Graciosa- The little pearl before Lanzarote

The 27 square kilometres small island La Graciosa is located on the north coast off Lanzarote. It was uninhabited until the end of the 19th century, after which a small fish factory was built and the first people settled. From that moment on the inhabitants overcame the difficult living conditions that an island without drinking water, with strong winds and land that was difficult to cultivate, brought with it. For years, traditional fishing was the only source of income that required crossing El Río, the strait between Lanzarote and La Graciosa, to sell the fish and use the proceeds to buy drinking water and other food.

For years, the islanders fought tenaciously for their island to officially become the "eighth island" of the archipelago. In October 2019 the goal was achieved and La Graciosa was recognised as the eighth island.

At present 748 people live on the island. In the summer months, about 4000 tourists join them. The manageable community owns an impressive 150 cars. In the "capital" Caleta de Sebo you will find a small medical centre, a post office, a pharmacy, a fish shop, the port administration, a health centre and 3 supermarkets. In the only island school, less than 40 children are taught. Recently, several restaurants and an aloe vera museum have opened.

La Graciosa [1] can already be seen from Lanzarote. From the Mirador del Río you can enjoy a fantastic view of the island, as well as of the uninhabited islands behind it, Montaña Clara, Roque del Oeste and Alegranza.

From Órzola you can take the ferry of Lineas Maritimas Romero. There are sufficient parking spaces at the jetty, which are allocated by parking attendants. The crossing takes only 30 minutes.

The first 10 minutes are, depending on the swell, a little wobbly, after the big rocks at the end of Lanzarote, the ship goes into shallower waters.

Once in the harbour you can explore the island on foot, by rental bike or guided by jeep.

On foot it is only 700 m to the first beach El Salado, which can be covered in 10 minutes.

The second beach, La Francesa, which is located in the south, can be reached in 40 minutes after 2.8 km, and the southernmost beach, Playa de La Cocina, can be reached in 55 minutes after 3.8 km.

The southernmost point of El Pobre can be reached after 7.4 km in 2 hours.

The El Corral depression, located in the west of the island, is 4 km away and can be reached from the main town in 1 hour and 10 minutes.

To the beach Las Conchas it is 5,1 km, for which you need 1 hour and 20 minutes. To Pedro Barba it is 6.4 km, which can be done in 1.4 hours.

By bike, the rental is directly opposite the jetty, it is of course faster, but you should remember that on the island there are only sandy tracks. So it takes 4 minutes to El Salado, 15 minutes to La Francesa, 30 minutes to El Corral, 35 minutes to Las Conchas, 40 minutes to Pedro Barba and 50 minutes to El Pobre. The jeep tours start on the right side of the harbour. There are single, return trips to the beaches, which, depending on the distance and number of people, can be obtained from the drivers.

6.1 La Graciosa- Complete island tour

The departure station of the jeeps is located in the harbour on the right-hand side. Not as indicated on the poster, the authorized drivers do the whole island tour for 50,00 €. The tour for the right or left side of the island costs 50,00 € each, for the whole tour 100,00 € are charged.

The whole island tour includes the following places:
- Pedro Barba
- Playa Lambra
- Caleton de los Arcos
- Playa de las Conchas - half of the island tour would go until here
- Baja Corral
- Caleton de las Hurtas
- Montaña Amarilla
- La Laguna
- Playa Francesa

The tour starts through the main town Caleta del Sebo of the island.

A sand road leads through the village to Pedro Baba, a tiny village with small houses that are only inhabited during the summer months. **Pedro Barba [2]** was the first inhabited place on the island. At the end of the small settlement there is a house which at that time housed a school for 4 pupils, behind it is the cemetery.

After a short break we continue towards Playa del Ambra. This part of the island is comparable to the snow-white dune landscape in Corralejo, in the north of Fuerteventura, but in miniature.

The next stop will be in front of Caleton de Los Arcos, where the guide will guide you on foot. The natural spectacle reminds on Los Hervideros in Lanzarote.

During the continuation of the drive in direction to Montaña Bermeja alongside the coast, the dream sand beach Playa de las Conchas is accessed.

The tour leads over the Baja del Corral and the Caleton de las Hutras to the Montaña Amarilla.

As the road does not go all the way around the island, the jeep drives the whole way back to the starting point with the new destination Playa Francesa.

Ferry times: www.lineasromero.com

Órzola- La Graciosa: 8.30/ 10.00/ 11.00/ 12.00/ 13.30/ 16.00/ 18.00 From 01 May to 31 October 19.00 and from 01 July to 20 October 20.00.

La Graciosa- Órzola: 8.00/ 8.40/ 10.00/ 11.00/ 12.30/ 15.00/ 16.00/ 17.00, and from 01 May to 31 October at 18.00 and from 01 July to 20 October at 19.00.

7   La Geria

La Geria [3] is a 5-hectare wine-growing area in the centre of the island, between the towns of Yaiza and San Bartolomé on the edge of the TimanfayaNational Park. It is the largest wine-growing area in the Canary Islands and has been declared a Nature Reserve.

During the heavy volcanic eruptions in the years 1730 to 1736 a layer of volcanic ash up to 2 m thick came down in this area. This layer of small lava stones is called Picón. It has the property that the little moisture that results from heavy cloud formation does not run off, but immediately seeps into the soil and can thus be absorbed by the plants.

This advantage was then and still is today used by the islanders for the cultivation of wine. In order to protect the vines from the continuous winds of varying force, a low wall of lava stones in the shape of a semicircle was built around each plant. Thus, the whole area of La Geria is covered by these stone semicircles, surrounded by vines in the middle, up to the volcanic mountains.

The same procedure is still used today to grow cereals and vegetables, except that outside this area the lava stones are poured into fields to make them usable. This is why you should not be surprised to find some big black lava fields outside of this area.

The impressive drive through the wine-growing area leads past many smaller and larger bodegas: El Campesino, El Grifo with wine museum, Stratus, Rubicon and La Geria.

Tip: Visit the winery, the Bodega Los Bermejos, with award-winning wines At the Monumento al Campesino turn left towards La Geria on the LZ-30. Shortly after the El Islote town sign, a fork in the road follows, with the indication of the winery.

Wine tastings are offered on request. Los Bermejos is available in white, rosé and red, as well as sparkling wine. According to many Lanzaroteños, it is the best wine of the island. Changing- Google, ☉◌ signposted, La Florida- LZ-30- Camino a los Bermejos,7- 35550 San Bartolomé

8   The Fire Mountains

8.1 *Sanctuary Ermita de Los Dolores*

The sanctuary **Ermita de Nuestra Señora de Los Dolores [4]** is considered the centre of Marian devotion in Lanzarote and is one of the most important in the Canary Islands. It is located in the town of Mancha Blanca, which belongs to the municipality of Tinajo.

According to history: In September 1730, the earth opened up in the Timanfaya area, and lava flows destroyed the villages and fertile valleys in this area. Volcanic eruptions began that lasted five years. In 1735 the glowing lava flows moved towards Tinajo via the village of Mancha Blanca.

Fearing that their houses would be destroyed, the inhabitants of the village marched towards the lava in a procession led by the parish priest Esteban de la Guardia with the statue of the Virgen de Los Dolores. One of the pilgrims rammed a heavy wooden cross into the earth in front of the lava flow and the lava came to a halt. Out of gratitude, the inhabitants of Tinajo vowed to build a pilgrimage church on this site of the Virgin. Years later the Virgin appeared to the shepherd girl Juana Rafaela and reminded her of this promise. In 1779 the inhabitants applied for permission to build the church, which was completed in 1782.

Every year the pilgrimage in honour of the Madonna takes place on 15 September. Since the proceedings are held on Saturdays, the date may be postponed by a few days.

In the church the priest holds Holy Mass, after which the statue is carried in front of the church, where the festivities begin.

The sleepy village is transformed on this day into a mixture of procession, fair and market.

Many Lanzaroteños dress in typical national costume for the pilgrimage Romería de Los Dolores and make the pilgrimage from their homes in groups on foot to Mancha Blanca.

In recent years, the colourful hustle and bustle has developed into an event with an attached small fair and several booths. Also the big artisan exhibition Feria de Artesania de Lanzarote takes place at the same time.

TIP: The small, simple church is definitely worth a visit, as it belongs to the history of the island. If you are on the island around September 15th, ask for the exact date of the Romeria and watch the spectacle. Also interesting is the handicraft market where not only the Lanzaroteños but also the inhabitants of the neighboured islands sell their works of art. ☻ Ermita all year round - daily, ⌂ Calle Virgen de los Dolores, 10- 35560 Tinajo

8.2   *Timanfaya Visitor Center- Centro de Visitantes*

An iron fire devil marks the beginning of the National Park Timanfaya. From the black lava masses, at the LZ-67, the big white visitor centre Centro de Visitantes stands out from the scree masses. The modern centre informs in a permanent exhibition about the volcanic island and offers much more than one would expect. 2 terraces lead you into untouched lava fields. From 09.45 - 14.45 hrs you will learn all about volcanic eruptions in a 40-minute film screening. The visual and acoustic simulation of the Timanfaya eruptions you should not miss the flaming **hell spectacle [5].** The German tour takes place at 10.30, 12.30 and 14.30 hours. ① The Tremesana hike starts from the Visitor Centre and can be booked exclusively via the Internet. 9 a.m. to 4 p.m. all year round, ◑⌂ LZ-67- 35560 Tinajo

8.3   *Tremesana- The hike through the National Park*

There is still misinformation that you can simply drive to the Centro de Visitantes, the visitor centre in Mancha Blanca, to walk through the national park.

I enquired at the office of the centre, whereupon I was informed that all the major guides had only made a written inquiry about the course of the hike, which was answered. In non-updated guides, this information is no longer applicable, as these were provided before the 1996s.

I had decided to take the **Tremesana Route [6]** in Spanish because there was exactly one place left. The English tour was already fully booked. When I arrived at the centre, after a short time the names of the participants were called up and you had to sign and enter your name, date of birth and passport number in a list, so I think it was in Spanish that you are physically fit. Since my name cannot be more German than German, the guide asked me when he called "Müller" and I sat down whether I was able to speak Spanish at all. After 10 sentences and some jokes it was clear that my Spanish, from his point of view, was sufficient.

And then it started. I got into the jeep, which was parked in front of the center, with my guide, a friendly sympathetic woman and the group, we were 8 people. The English-speaking group sat next to it in the 2nd jeep.

We drove towards Timanfaya, past the camels, destination Yaiza. Already during the departure, the travel guide reports in detail about the history of Lanzarote and the volcanic eruptions. Arriving in Yaiza, they went along a bumpy road until they reached a barrier, which they opened to enter the national park. The jeep was parked and our hike began.

Super interesting and informative, halfway we met the English guided group.

One could ask questions, the group stopped at especially interesting places and the guide gave a knowledge that I had not heard before. For example, a huge monolith, which is located next to Montaña Colorada, where I have been several times, was hurled 20 km.

What I also did not know up to now is that one must not walk carelessly over the lava fields that are stuck, for example in the area of the Monumento al Campesino, as the lava could have thrown bubbles underground and as soon as the lava layer is too thin, one could collapse and get injured.

The excursion ended after about 2 hours at the height of El Golfo, where we got into the jeep of the other group and drove back to the centre.

My conclusion: the Tremesana-hiking tour that is made for free through the national park is an absolute must for Lanzarote fans and those who still want to become one. A real experience!

Unfortunately the tours are only offered in English and Spanish. A fluent Spanish is required for the Spanish tour, a "Hola, que tal?" is not sufficient. Moreover, it would be a pity and unfair to the committed employees of the national park to miss the information.

Important to know: Visit the website of the National Park at www.reservasparquesnacionales.es and select the route.

Reservations can only be made up to 2 months in advance, depending on capacity utilization. Age of participants: from 16 years.

8.4   *Timanfaya Fire Mountains- Montañas del Fuego*

The fire mountains **Montañas del Fuego [7]** also called Timanfaya, are located in the southwest of the island and belong to a large area affected by volcanic eruptions between 1730 and 1736 and later in 1824. This long, eruptive process drastically changed the appearance of the island. Almost a quarter of Lanzarote was buried under a thick layer of lava and ashes.

The volcanic landscape has a total circumference of 174 square kilometres, but the part protected as a national park, where the most significant eruptions took place, occupies an area of only 51 square kilometres. This extends in the east from the city limit of Yaiza to the Montaña Timanfaya, the western limit forms the coast. Here 32 volcanic cones were created.

The special climatic conditions of the island led to the fact that the volcanic landscape is almost unchanged and the Timanfaya area was declared a national park in 1974.

Between 1726 and 1730 there were strong earthquakes and underground rumbling, which caused panic among the inhabitants. In search of shelter they went to Teguise and Arrecife. The eruption began towards the end of the summer of 1730, on the evening of September 1st. The events of that time are recorded in the chronicles of an extraordinary eyewitness, the parish priest of Yaiza Don Andres Lorenzo Curbelo.

He described: "Between nine and ten o'clock in the evening, the earth suddenly opened up near Timanfaya, only two miles from Yaiza.During the first night, a huge mountain rose from the bosom of the earth and flames escaped from its summit and burned for 19 days".

This was the beginning of the most important volcanic process of the Canary Islands. It lasted for six years with varying intensity and was marked by lava flows, with a temperature of more than 800O and huge ash showers that wiped out all life.

In the historical manuscript of the parish priest the following report can be read: "On October 18th 1730, three new openings were formed over Santa Catalina and from them steam masses arose, which spread all over the island, accompanied by cinders and ashes which were spread all over the area. The explosions that accompanied these phenomena, the darkness produced by the masses of ash and the smoke that enveloped the entire island drove the inhabitants of Yaiza to flee more than once".

Today, almost 300 years later, more and more life pulsates in the middle of the lava. About 800 animal and plant species were registered. Most of them on land, the rest at sea. Among the organisms that live directly on the rocks are mainly birds, lizards and above all various species of lichens, as well as some nocturnal insects that feed on microscopic particles carried by the wind. These are mainly beetles and crickets, which may have been very similar to the species that arrived on the island millions of years ago when Lanzarote emerged from the sea.

The last volcanic eruptions took place in 1824. They were preceded by a 10-year period during which numerous medium intensity earthquakes were recorded on the island. The peculiarities of these eruptions were the thin fluidity of the lava and the enormous columns of boiling saltwater that gushed out of the craters at a height of up to 30 metres and flooded the area.

During this phase the last of the lava flows threatened the village of Mancha Blanca. Out of necessity, the inhabitants borrowed the statue of the Virgen de Los Dolores, the church in the neighbouring village of Tinajo. And the miracle happened. A wooden cross was rammed into the glowing lava, which came to a halt shortly afterwards.

8.5 Island Hilario- Islote de Hilario

Along the Timanfaya, unusual temperatures developed on the surface, originating from the earth, which volcanologists call geothermal anomalies. The centre is located at the top of the island of Hilario, where several demonstrations are presented to the spectators.

According to legend, the island takes its name from Hilario from Lanzarote, who lived there alone with his camel mare like a hermit. Hilario planted a fig treethat flourished but never bore fruit because "the flower could not feed on the flame".

A tribute to the legend can be found in the restaurant El Diablo: inside you will see an open, glazed circle with camel bones and the branches of a **fig tree [8]** on black picon.

8.6 Timanfaya- Volcano Route- La Ruta de los Volcanes

Inside the **national park [1] there** is a 14 km long route that is exclusively used by bus. It was realized in 1968 under the direction of César Manrique and Jésus Soto. The line of the road is harmoniously adapted to the landscape and runs along the volcanic eruption zone. On this impressive tour you will see small ovens, caves and heavily eroded dry barren land.

➀ After arriving in Timanfaya National Park by car and paying the entrance fee, drive up to the collective parking lot. There you will board the buses of the National Park with your entrance ticket to be driven through the unique volcanic landscape. Contrary to some assertions, there is no other possibility. Guests who are travelling with organised bus trips will only get back on their coach, which will be travelling the same route.

8.7 Timanfaya- Restaurant El Diablo

In 1970, the **restaurant El Diablo [2] was** built under the direction of César Manrique at the exact point where the thermal anomalies are most severe. It is located on Islote del Hilario in TimanfayaNational Park and was built before the area was declared a National Park.

Cooking is done with natural geothermal energy. The kitchen stove is a six-meter-deep hole in the form of a well from which heat rises to cook the barbecue on a large grate. Only materials that can withstand the high temperatures were used for the construction. In the circular restaurant you can enjoy a fantastic view of the Timanfaya area through the large windows.

Specialities include half, grilled chicken, sardines, marinated chicken legs, chicken breast, mixed skewers, entrecôte, fillet of beef and lamb chops. Important: A visit to the restaurant is only possible in connection with the entrance fee for the National Park.

8.8   TimanfayaNational Park - on your own or organised?

Basically there are two possibilities to visit the fire mountains: On your own in a rental car or with an organized bus tour.

Depending on the rush of visitors, there can be long queues of cars after the ticket booth in the park, so that one has to be prepared for waiting times of up to nearly one hour. It is easier with the coach, because they are let through immediately.

After the ticket office, drive up to the parking lot, park the car and walk towards the restaurant, before the screening by National Park employees takes place.

In order to demonstrate the immense heat of the earth, you will be given small stones in your hand. Afterwards, gorse is burned and impressive water fountains are released from burrows.

At the end of the demonstration, you will be taken to a giant barbecue, on which chicken legs, skewers and sausages are grilled in a six-metre deep well using only geothermal energy.

Guests of the organized trips return to the coaches, the drivers change to the collective buses of the National Park. Unfortunately, it is no longer possible to drive through the area by yourself. Before departure the bus driver will validate the ticket. Then follows a 45-minute journey through the fascinating Timanfaya landscape. The route to be taken by the organised coach or by the collective bus is identical.

In the Timanfaya- collecting bus a 3-language CD with the history of the volcanic eruptions is inserted with musical background. The languages are Spanish, English and German.

Arrived at the final station there is still the possibility to shop in the souvenir shop. In most cases, the guided tours leave their guests 30 minutes to continue their journey.

The situation is different for those who are travelling with their own vehicle. If you feel like it, you can watch the fire shows again, or you can go for a meal in the restaurant "El Diablo".

8.9   Camel ride - Echadero de los Camellos

The camel resting place **Echadero de los Camellos [3]** is located on the main road leading through the Timanfayanature reserve.

Immediately you will see waiting camels, or rather dromedaries and caravans, which make their way with tourists on the humps to be rocked through the lava landscape for a fee.

On the right-hand side of the parking lot there is a small snack café with the possibility to buy souvenirs, public toilets, and a small free exhibition on the subject: Timanfaya and camels - how the animals were used to make farming work easier. ☉ Daily 9 a.m. to 4 p.m., ⌂ LZ-67

① Alternatively, you can also take a camel ride at Lanzarote Safari, where you will also receive a "camel driving licence" with photo and as a gift a hat.☉ Daily 10.30-17.30, in summer until 18.30, www. lanzarotesafari.com, ⌂ LZ-2, km 17, 35570 Uga

9   Lago Verde- Laguna de los Clicos

Shortly before the fishing village of El Golfo is the Lago Verde with the **Laguna de los Clicos [4]**. To discover the "green lake", drive down the road to El Golfo and park on the left just before entering the town.

At the end of the parking lot the path begins, which leads uphill to the lake after about 10 minutes.

The lagoon is crescent-shaped in the arch of a partially submerged volcanic crater, about thirty metres from the coast. The lake owes its bright green colour to the influence of the Ruppia Maritima algae, which find optimal living conditions in the extremely salty water of the lagoon.

Although the lagoon is connected to the sea underground and is constantly being replenished with fresh seawater, it is evaporating more and more and has already lost a considerable part of its original size. The lake has been placed under nature protection and is cordoned off with ropes. Entering and bathing is prohibited. Nevertheless, you should not miss the colourful natural spectacle.

In the adjacent fishing village El Golfo, countless restaurants invite you to eat fish. ☉ Daily, ⌂ LZ-703

10   Los Hervideros

On the southwest coast, between the Janubio salt flats and the fishing village of El Golfo, are the bizarre rock formations of **Los Hervideros [5]**.

Hervidero means "bubbling", so it is obvious why this stretch of coast is called so. Especially when the rough high waves of the Atlantic hit the rock masses, it seems as if the water is still boiling.

The landscape was created during the last great volcanic eruptions between 1730 and 1736, when the hot lava masses of the Timanfaya poured into the sea and solidified rapidly.

On narrow paths you reach the small, extended platforms from which you can watch the spectacle from close up.

Only when the surf is strong can you experience a fantastic natural spectacle of the approaching waves that force their way through the rock slabs and shoot into the air as meter-high fountains. In the background the high volcanic craters of the Montañas del Fuego impress. ☉ Daily, ⌂ LZ-703

11   Salt flats of Janubio- Las Salinas de Janubio

In Lanzarote, there are only two salt works left. To the north are the Salinas del Río, to the west the **Salinas de Janubio [6]**. At the top of the main street you have a wonderful view over the whole complex.

The Janubio salt flats are the largest in the Canary Islands and are among the most important in the world. They have existed since 1895 and were designed by the salt mine worker Victor Fernandez. The complex was built from volcanic rock and is under monumental protection.

At that time the water was taken from the lagoon by 5 windmills with paddle wheels, which stood on stone bases of different heights. In the meantime this is done by electric motors.

The water runs through a main channel and reaches the different evaporation basins via side channels. This is followed by repeated decanting into other basins, which increases the original salt content from 4 to 20 %. The water is then transferred to crystallization tanks. After about 3 weeks the salt separates from the brine.

This process is repeated up to 14 times between March and October. The salt is dried and cleaned in lateral ditches until the next flooding of the basin. From November to February, repair work is carried out on the plant.

Through the open entrance gate you go down to the salt bodega Bodega de la Sal.

On the right side you can see the salt flats from the slightly elevated platform. A guided tour of the salt works with subsequent salt tasting is offered.☉ Mon- Fr 10.30/ 12 o'clock, in German and English, ♨12 €, ⓘwww. salinasdejanubio.com

In 2019, the company had its sea salt tested for quality by an independent institute. The laboratory certified that neither

microplastic parts nor impurities can be detected in the salt. The "Flor de Sal", which was awarded the gold medal in November 2019, deserves special mention.
Tip: Take advantage of the large selection of salt in the local bodega.

be offered: Sea salt with volcanic activated carbon, aromatic herbs, chilli, lemon, Tenerife Guayonje-onion, tomato, or red wine. Seasoning salts for meat, fish, pasta and vegetables.
Sal Malvasía Volcánica- with Malsavía- wine and herbs
Sal condimentada al Mojo picón extra hot with garlic, caraway, pepperoni and hot peppers
Sal condimentada al Cúrcuma- with turmeric, garlic and oregano
Sal condimentada al tomillo with thyme, garlic and oregano
Sal al Vino tinto with red wine and herbs
Sal al Mojo picón- with spicy peppers, chillies and garlic
Sal condimentada al Curry- with curry, garlic and oregano
Sal condimentada al Mojo verde- with parsley, coriander, garlic and green pepper.
❂ Mon- Fr 10-17 h, Sat 11-16 h, Sun closed, ⌂ LZ-2> LZ-703 > signposted

12   Lanzarote- Fuerteventura

Two islands that are so close together and could not be more different. Already from Puerto del Carmen and many viewpoints you can see the snow-white dunes of Corralejo on **Fuerteventura [7]**.
This is not surprising, as Fuerteventura is only 15 km away from Lanzarote. There are several ways to see the snow-white sand, the huge sand dunes and the **turquoise water [8]:**
The easiest is to book an organized excursion with the destination Fuerteventura- Corralejo and the dunes. The glass-bottomed boat takes you from the harbour in Playa Blanca to Fuerteventura. Most of the times, a shopping stop is made in the centre of Corralejo, after which one is taken with the group in the bus to the dunes and the beach. After another period of availability with the possibility to swim, one is brought back to the harbour of Corralejo, crosses again by boat and is taken to the hotels of Lanzarote.
The second possibility would be that you go to Fuerteventura on your own with the car ferries of Armas or Fred Olsen, each in only 30 minutes, or with the glass bottom boat in about 45-minutes. Once you arrive in Fuerteventura, take a taxi from the port or take the public bus to the dunes. The bus station is located directly at the back of the harbour building.

ⓘ🚌 www.tiadhe.com, Bus 6, exit bus stop 146 HOTELES RIU, entry bus stop 141.

The taxi prices are humane, as the dunes are not too far away.

If you have already rented a car in Lanzarote, depending on the car rental company, there is the option to take the car to Fuerteventura for a day. This would be the easiest and most independent way to explore the island, but the price for the crossing plus car should be considered and compared with the ferry companies.

ⓘ www.navieraarmas.com or www.fredolsen.es

For the crossing you need an identity card or passport.

Conclusion: If you have never been to Fuerteventura, you should in any case have a look at the Canarian favourite island of the German beach vacationers. The huge snow-white dune landscape around Corralejo and the turquoise water alone are a feast for the eyes. To get to the beaches, follow the signs for Playas Grandes. Here are some of the most beautiful beaches of the north, which are located in front of the RIU Tres Islas and the RIU Oliva Beach.

Unfortunately, it is not possible to explore Fuerteventura sufficiently in one day with a rented car, as the island is too long. From the northernmost point in Corralejo to the southernmost point in Morro Jable it takes more than 2 hours, which is only possible without any stop. This is why I recommend to stay in the north of Fuerteventura and enjoy a nice day at the beach. Do not forget your swimsuit!

13 César Manrique- a unique artist

Today's Lanzarote would be unthinkable without the enormous influence of César Manrique. He was not only a painter, architect, sculptor, but also an active environmentalist and had a decisive influence on the image of the volcanic island. It is thanks to him that the beauty of Lanzarote has not been lost in mass tourism, but has been highlighted by a harmonious combination of art and nature.

César Manrique [1] was born on 24 April 1919 in Arrecife. He grew up with his twin sister, his brother and another sister in Puerto Naos, the old port of Arrecife. A carefree childhood and summer holidays with his family in Caleta de Famara, a small fishing village in the northwest, had a lasting effect on him. During the Spanish Civil War, from July 1936 to April 1939, Manrique volunteered to fight alongside Franco, later dictator General Francisco Franco. After the war he returned to Arrecife, immediately banished his uniform and never again spoke a word about the cruel wartime and the memories associated with it.

Already in 1942, at the age of 23, he presented works in his first exhibition in the capital of the island. He enrolled in Tenerife, in the oldest university of the Canary Islands, in the field of technical architecture and after 2 years he dropped out of his studies.

In 1950, after five years of study, he completed his second degree at the Academy of Fine Arts in Madrid with the title of Master of Drawing and Painting. He married Pepi Gomez with whom he maintained a close relationship until her death in 1963.

Together with like-minded artists, Manrique developed into a pioneer of avant-garde art and opened Spain's first gallery for abstract art in Madrid in 1954.

In 1964, at the age of 45, he received a scholarship from the International Institute of Art Education in America. In New York, three exclusive solo exhibitions took place in the gallery "Catherine Viviano".

For his further development as an artist, representatives of abstract expressionism, as well as pop art (Andy Warhol), new sculpture and kinetic art were decisive. After a 4 year stay in the USA, he was homesick in 1966 and decided to return to Lanzarote to turn his home island into one of the most beautiful places in the world.

Already in Tenerife and Gran Canaria, a merciless building boom in form of huge hotel castles and interventions into the landscape had taken place that now also threatened to destroy Lanzarote. Manrique was able to win over a long-time friend of the family, Pepin Ramirez, who had become president of the island government, for his project. Only the traditional, maximum two-storey construction should be allowed and a ban on advertising posters on the island should be introduced. This ban was enforced, but has since been lifted.

In order to pass on the Lanzarote architectural style to his fellow countrymen, Manrique took the initiative and drove his car across the island in order to convince everybody of the original architecture.

In the same year he designed the Monumento al Campesino, the 15-metre-high monument to working farmers, welded together from the water tanks of old fishing boats. His closest partner Jésus Soto realized the monument.

Together with his artist friend Luis Ibánez, he bought an old house in Yaiza, one of three that had been left standing after the volcanic eruptions of 1730 to 1736, and converted it into the La Era Restaurant in 1970.

In the same year, he discovered a fig tree in a black lava field in Tahiche, thegreen top of which protruded from a lava flow. He decided to build his house exactly on this spot. The landowners did not demand payment for their land because they considered it worthless and asked Manrique to take as much land as he needed for his project. During the construction phase, Manrique discovered five underground lava bubbles, which he connected, expanded and converted into living quarters.

In 1974, Manrique opened the multi-purpose cultural centre EL Almacen in Arrecife, which was intended to serve as a meeting place for people interested in art. Artists should be given the opportunity to exhibit their works in the El Aljibe art gallery.

In 1982 he created his foundation, the Fundacíon César Manrique.

In 1988, he moved out of the house in Tahiche to move to his converted farmhouse in Haría, which has been a museum since 2013. On 25 September 1992, César Manrique diedin a traffic accident only 50 metres from his foundation in Tahiche. At the crossroads where he had passed a stop sign, there is now a roundabout with a wind chime designed by him. He was buried in the cemetery of Haría. His twin sister died on 13.11.2018.

The following buildings, designed by César Manrique, can be visited

The Casa Museo del Campesino, a **complex of farmhouses [2]** in typical island architecture with the **Monumento al Campesino [3]**, a monument that stands at the geographical centre of the island to honour the farmers of Lanzarote who discovered that the black lava stones are porous and so the dew can be absorbed to irrigate the fields.

The **Lagomar [4]**, the residential complex of Omar Sharif and the viewpoint **Mirador del Río [5]** with a view of the neighbouring island La Graciosa.

The **Jameos del Agua [6]**, a lagoon inside a lava cave that houses a blind albino crab, a concert hall with 600 seats and the cactus garden, the **Jardín de Cactus [7]**, with more than 1000 cactus species.

The **Fundación César Manrique [8]**, his house with 5 underground lava bubbles and his last residence the **Casa/ Museo César Manrique [9]**.

The **restaurant El Diabolo [10]** in the National Park Timanfaya, in the middle of the active fire mountains, with a large grill over volcanic air and the **Castillo San José [11]** with the Museo Internacional de Arte Contemporaneo, a contemporary museum with changing art exhibitions and the integrated restaurant Que Muac.

In Costa Teguise, César Manrique designed the fishing village Pueblo Marinero in the centre and was responsible for the design of the green and pool area in the **Hotel Meliá Las Salinas [12]**. He expressed his creativity in the wind chimes **Juegetes del Viento**

[13], which can be found in his Fundación and on many roundabouts on the island.

14   Las Playas

Lanzarote is not the beach paradise with endlessly long and bright sand beaches. Due to the tides of the Atlantic Ocean all beaches can be used, but in many cases bathing is only possible at high tide.

At low tide, the sea recedes so far that sometimes only black stones or black lava flows that go into the sea remain. So the so-called "beach life" has two faces in most cases. At high tide, a wow-effect is created, so that one is happy about the crystal-clear sea and turquoise play of colours. On the other hand, at low tide, when the black, thick stones appear in the sea, one thinks that a truck has driven up and unloaded the debris.

By this way, many vacationers who are in Lanzarote for the first time say that this is not what they imagined at all and that everything is terribly terrible. Nevertheless, both high and low tide have their own special visual appeal.

In Lanzarote, most of the beaches are made of fine sand, a few are coarse or a mixture of sand and stones. Most of the times, one finds light sand, but there are also brown and black sand beaches.

In the holiday regions Costa Teguise, Puerto del Carmen, Playa Blanca and in the capital, sunbeds and parasols are offered for a fee. Between the set up sunbathing areas there is enough space to sit down with your own beach sheet. Only here you should go swimming, because lifeguards are on duty. Please never underestimate the extremely strong undercurrents of the Atlantic Ocean, which cost countless lives every year.

Water temperatures are around 24o from July to September and can drop to 17o in the winter months.

The outside temperatures are highest in summer, reaching 35o in the shade during the day and dropping to 25o in the evening. Tolerable by a, depending on weather conditions mild or strong wind, a fleece jacket is recommended in the evening hours.

In the summer months the UV value is 12, in the winter months 4- 5. Do not underestimate this radiation and protect yourself with a sunscreen with a sufficient sun protection factor. Caution is required, because the wind usually makes you notice how aggressive the sun is much too late.

One of the absolute highlights are the natural seawater basins **Piscinas Naturales [1]** in Punta Mujeres to the north. On the 2 km long sandy beachless coastal section, small bathing bays have been created, which are especially popular with the locals during the summer months. Here, you step outside the door with bath slippers and a towel to refresh yourself in the cool waters of the Atlantic Ocean. Along the promenade you will find the small bathing bays Playa Grande, El Muro, El Cura and Las Rosas. Only a small amount of construction work was done with railings, ladders and small concrete sun terraces. The rest is pure landscape and fishing village atmosphere. ⌂ LZ-1, signposted

Further north, after the Jameos del Agua, towards Órzola, there are eight different coves. As these beaches are located outside the tourist centres, you have to travel by car.

The coastal stretch in this zone belongs to the Malpais de la Corona. It is characterized by a low rocky coast with small bays and snow-white sand and contrasts fantastically with the black volcanic landscape. A feast for the eyes that is second to none. In places, the bright bays have dug into the black landscape and continue inland in the form of white dunes. ⌂ LZ-1

Playa del **Caleton Blanco [2]** is the largest of these bays. The snow-white sandy beach is about five hundred meters long. There are no deckchairs, but there are semicircular walls made of stacked lava stones, in which you can lie down protected from the wind.

Tip: Those who want to spend the day here should also take a sunshade, towels, sun lotion and drinks.

Unfortunately during the summer months the beautiful bathing bay with a view of Órzola and Monte Corona is very crowded. The Lanzaroteños spend a whole weekend here with their children, camping and barbecue. Please note that you can only swim here at high tide, as the sea is only knee-deep when the tide is absolutely low.⓵ The car can be parked directly in front of the beach, ⌂ LZ-1, KM 32

The lonely **Playa del Risco** is located below the Salinas del Río.

If one is right in front of the Mirador del Río, one turns left into the narrow street. On the right-hand side you have a wonderful view of the island La Graciosa off Lanzarote. The road is quite straight and curving downhill. Shortly after an old building, the first one on the right side, a right-left curve follows, on the left side you can see a hotel finca. Exactly after this bend, just before the finca, after a green lava accumulation covered with lichens, you turn right before the electricity pylons begin.

If you see a jerky path with black cobbled lava stones, you are in the right place. Now you drive the way to the end and park the car. Then, unfortunately, comes the most difficult part. The approximately one kilometre long and lonely beach is very difficult to access. At least you should wear sneakers, even better would be hiking boots, otherwise you can only reach the upper platform, which is about 15 minutes away.

After that the path goes down steep and scree without railings. According to two sporty, young men, the descent to the beach takes an hour. The way back is accordingly more difficult and takes one and three-quarters of an hour. You should at least have a look at Playa del Risco from the platform that is still relatively easy to reach. By the way, the men found it "so amazing", but said that you only have to do something like that once in a lifetime, so that a repetition was ruled out. ⌂ LZ-201> LZ-203> at the Mirador after about 3.2 km> Las Rositas,2 - 35541 Haría

Playa de Famara [3] is an almost three kilometre long beach with light brown sand, located at the foot of the Famara cliffs. Due to a high swell and strong winds it is mainly used by kite and windsurfers. ⌂ LZ-402

Playa La Santa Sport [4] is an almost one kilometre long, artificially created, light-coloured sandy beach near the sports facilities of Club La Santa. ⌂ LZ-410

The beaches or rocky coast with bathing platforms **Charco del Palo** and **Los Cocoteros, located at the** level of the cactus garden, are nudist zones. ⌂ LZ-1> LZ-1A >signposted

At the **Costa Teguise there are** five bathing bays of different sizes that are all located at the boardwalk.

Playa Ancla [5], a small bathing bay, is located in front of the big Occidental Hotel Lanzarote Beach, at the entrance of the village. ⌂ Avenida El Salinero,6- 35508 Costa Teguise

Playa Bastian [6] is located at the beginning of Costa Teguise, directly on the promenade. The 400 m long beach with dark sand is mostly used by locals. ⌂ Calle La Rosa- 35508 Costa Teguise

The **Playa de Jabillo [7]** is a small bathing bay with a light-coloured sandy beach that is streaked with rocks and is located at the promenade in front of the Occidental Grand Hotel Teguise. ⌂ Avenida del Jabillo, 35508 Costa Teguise

The **Playa de las Cucharas [8]** is the largest beach on the Costa Teguise. The light sandy beach of about 600 meters is divided by a long breakwater that runs perpendicular to the bay. This means that swimming in the sea is also possible at low tide. The section to the left of the breakwater, in front of the Hotel Melía Salinas, turns into a sea of black stones at low tide. ⌂ Avenida Arenas Blancas, 35508 Costa Teguise

The **Playa de los Charcos [9]** is located directly in front of the Hotel Lanzarote Beach and has a light sandy beach. Due to cooled lava flows, swimming in the sea is only possible at high tide. ⌂ Calle del Mástil- 35508 Costa Teguise

In the **Arrecife** area you will find two beaches. The **Playa del Reducto [10]** is the 500 m long city beach of Arrecife, which is located directly next to the Grand Hotel Arrecife on the promenade. The beautiful light-coloured sandy beach with turquoise water invites you to swim at high tide. ⌂ Avenida Fred Olsen- 35509 Arrecife

Playa de Guasimeta [11] is an almost two-kilometre-long beach with fine, light brown sand in Playa Honda. It is located between Arrecife and the airport and is mainly used by islanders and residents. ⌂ Avenida Playa Honda, 35509 Playa Honda

In the area of Puerto del Carmen there are 3 big sand beaches:

The **Playa de Matagorda [12] is** located in front of the settlement of Matagorda and is a light brown sandy beach, which is interspersed with stones. ⌂ Calle Agunal- 35510 Puerto del Carmen

The **Playa de Los Pocillos [13] is** located shortly before Puerto del Carmen on the beach promenade and is a very deep brown sandy beach over one kilometre long. ⌂ Avenida de las Playas, 35510 Puerto del Carmen The **Playa Grande [14]** is the main beach of Puerto del Carmen with light brown sand, which passes directly under the promenade in Puerto del Carmen. ⌂ Avenida de las Playas, 35510 Puerto del Carmen

At the end of Puerto del Carmen is the small bay **Playa Chica [15]**. ⌂ Paseo Barrilla, 35510 Puerto del Carmen

Playa de Quemada [16] is a dark stone beach, which is located in the village of Playa Quemada. From here, one can get to Playa Blanca in five to six hours by a hiking path that passes two further bays. ⌂ LZ-2> LZ-706

In the south of the island there are the Papagayo beaches **Playas de Papagayo [17]**, which consist of the bays Playa Mujeres, Playa del Pozo, Playa de la Cera, Puerto Muela and Caleta del Congrio. The 100- 400m long light sand beaches are separated from each other by high cliffs. ⌂ LZ-702> roundabout> signposted, 35580 Playa Blanca A ⓞlong, bumpy gravel road leads to a cash box with a barrier, 3 € per 🔒vehicle, then the road leads to the beaches.

In the place Playa Blanca you meet 3 further bath bays. The **Playa Dorada [18]** is 200 m long and is located directly in front of the Hotel Princesa Yaiza. **Playa Flamingo [19]** is a bay protected by square concrete blocks, located in front of the Hotel Iberostar

Selection Lanzarote Park. The small city beach is located in the centre of the village. ⌂ Avenida Maritima- 35580 Playa Blanca

In the southwest of the island there are further beaches between the Salinas de Janubio and El Golfo where one can only bath at one's own risk. **Playa de Janubio [20]** is a long, dark sandy beach that separates the salt flats from the sea. After Los Hervideros follows the **Charco de los Clicos [21]** with a small lake and a black stone beach at the end of El Golfo. ⌂ LZ-2> LZ-703

15   Shopping - Shopping

Lanzarote is not a shopping paradise that would make the heart of a confirmed shopping lover beat faster. In the big holiday resorts Costa Teguise, Puerto del Carmen and Playa Blanca you will find mainly souvenir shops, in the small shopping centres, the Centros Comerciales, Chinese and Indians offer plagiarisms of current brands. On beaches and promenades the same is done by African vendors.

You can buy branded goods, which are only available in specialist shops, either in the capital Arrecife or in the large shopping centres.

The largest shopping centre **DEILAND [1] is** located between Arrecife and the airport on the LZ-2 motorway.

You can find all current shops at: www.deilandplaza.com/tiendas/

The **BIOSFERA PLAZA [2]** in Puerto del Carmenis the second largest shopping centre.

You can find all current shops at: www.biosferaplaza.es

In the port of **Puerto Calero [3] there is** a small, manageable shopping street with more exclusive brand shops.

You can find the current transactions at: www.caleromarinas.com

In the south of the island, the **MARINA RUBICON** shopping centre **[4]** was renovated and reopened.

On the ground floor there are several specialist shops, but in the marina you can shop more extensively. You can find all current shops at: www.ccmarinalanzarote.com/tiendas/

① On 1 October 2015 H&M opened its first store on Lanzarote in the Deiland shopping centre. The well-known sports shop Decathlon was added with a large hall in Arrecife, at the LZ-3- exit 4, in October 2016.

Important for shopping in the capital Arrecife are the opening hours, which differ from those of the shopping centres. As a rule, the shops are open from Monday to Friday from 10.00 to 14.00, after the lunch break from 17.00 to 20.00 and on Saturdays from 10.00 to 14.00.

We're closed on Sundays. The shopping centres are open daily from 10.00 to 22.00 hours.

Note: Just like in Germany, the stores carry spring, summer, autumn and winter collections. For summer clothing you can find real bargains from mid-August, the winter sales start on 06 January and end at the beginning of March. Oversizes for ladies are available at H&M as well as from the Spanish companies Encuentro up to size 46 and Punta Roma up to size 54.

TIP: You can find chic Spanish fashion at affordable prices in the Deiland shopping centre at the Cortefiel chain, which also offers a more exclusive collection under Pedro del Hierro. You can take a look at the collection on the website: www.cortefiel.com

15.1 Tobacco products- cigarettes

Tobacco products are available in supermarkets and tobacco shops. Even if the prices on the plane seem cheap, they are cheaper locally. Due to the low taxation, the price per bar starts at about 17,00 €. Cigarette packs sold individually or from the vending machine are a little more expensive, as there is no price labelling.

Important: On the return journey to Germany, only 1 pole per person over 18 years of age may be imported. In order to pass through customs without any problems, please make sure that there is only 1 bar in the suitcase, as the luggage is considered personal.

15.2 Perfumeries- Profumerías

Perfume and cosmetic products are also much cheaper in the Canarian Islands than in Germany. In order not to be fooled by plagiarism, you should buy in perfumeries and compare prices beforehand.

15.3 Pharmacy- Farmacia

Nearly all drugs are cheaper than in Germany. Even without a prescription, you can get the medicine without any problems in an opened box.

15.4 Food

In the holiday areas you will find small supermarkets of the chains Spar and Dino almost on every corner, where you can find everything you need in addition to the hotel offer. Larger purchases at lower prices are better made in the large branches of the Spanish chains EuroSpar, Hiperdino or Mercadona. The German supermarket chain

LIDL is represented on Lanzarote with 3 branches in Arrecife, in Playa Honda and in Puerto del Carmen.

15.5 Value Added Tax

The prices indicated in the shops are final prices. Please note that for food and drinks in bars and restaurants, if not specified, an additional 7% VAT will be added to the indicated price. Hotels and Manrique Tourist Centres only show the final price on the food and drink menus.

15.6 Marina Lanzarote

In 2014 the building complex Marina Lanzarote was opened on the outskirts of the capital Arrecife. The modern marina is a combination of restaurants and shops, which passes the marina. The complex can be reached on foot from the city via a bridge. When cruise ships arrive, the masses push past the marina. Apart from that, there are neither tourists nor locals to be seen, so that meanwhile many shops and restaurants are empty. Only the Burger King and the discotheque Kopas, which is open for party-goers on weekends from midnight, will be visited. ⌂ Avenida Olof Palme,35500 Arrecife

16   Overview markets- Mecados- Mercadillos

Daily you can visit markets on the island.

Monday through Saturday:
◉Mon-Fri 8- 22.30, Sat 8-15, ⌂ Calle de la Liebre/ Calle Manuel Miranda, 35500 Arrecife
The weekly market "La Recova" is located in the old market hall of Arrecife. Local food and handicrafts are offered.

Tuesdays:
◉ 9:30-14, ⌂ Avenida del Mar, 35508 Costa Teguise
The farmer's market in the Pueblo Marinero in Costa Teguise consists of several small stalls selling fruit, vegetables, olives, goat cheese, wine and bananas.

◉10-14, ⌂ Calle Pantalanes, 35570 Puerto Calero
In the marina of Puerto Calero you will find a colourful market with plagiarism and handicrafts.

Wednesdays:
🕐10-14, ⌂ Calle Berrugo, 35580 Playa Blanca
Against the backdrop of the marina you can shop at countless stands. From plagiarism to arts and crafts, you are sure to find the right souvenir here.

🕐18-22.30, ⌂ Avenida del Mar, 35508 Costa Teguise
In the evening hours you will meet craftsmen.

Thursdays:
🕐9-14, ⌂ **Calle** Miguel Hernandez, 3550 Tahíche
In front of the cultural centre Centro Cultural Santiago del Mayor there is a small farmers' market with fresh local produce.

Fridays:
🕐10-14, ⌂ **Pedestrian zone** Calle Léon y Castillo, 35500 Arrecife
In the capital's pedestrian zone, artisans await you next to the open shops and cafés.

🕐10-14, ⌂ Calle Pantalanes, 35570 Puerto Calero
In the marina of Puerto Calero you will find a colourful market with plagiarism and handicrafts.

🕐4-22pm, ⌂Avenida del Veradero, 35518 Puerto del Carmen
On the big market you will find everything your heart desires.

🕐6-22pm, ⌂ Avenida del Mar, 35508 Costa Teguise
In the evening hours you will meet craftsmen.

Saturdays:
🕐9- 2pm, ⌂ Calle Joaquin Rodriguez, 35570 Uga
Next to the small church you will meet local food and craftsmen.

🕐9-13, ⌂ Plaza de las Palmas,1- 35500 Arrecife
Around the square of the parish church of San Ginés there are stalls with fresh, local products.

🕐10-14, ⌂ Calle Berrugo, 35580 Playa Blanca
Against the backdrop of the marina you can shop at countless stands. From plagiarism to arts and crafts, you are sure to find the right souvenir here.

🕐10- 2 pm, ⌂ Calle Sol- 35520 Haría

After many years, the handicraft market in front of the church in the centre of Haría has become a real highlight.

Sundays:
◔9- 2 pm, ⌂ Calle Joaquin Rodrìguez- 35570 Uga
At the edge of the wine growing area La Geria, the small farmers' market presents local food and a selection of handicrafts.

◔10- 2pm, ⌂ Centre- 35530 Teguise
At the island's most important market you can buy plagiarisms, souvenirs and handicrafts at well over 500 stalls. There is also a lot on offer for the palate.

◔10- 1 pm, ⌂ Calle Virgen de los Dolores- 35560 Mancha Blanca
Opposite the church Nuestra Señora de Los Dolores farmers offer local products.

16.1 Teguise Market - Mercadillo Teguise

The **Mercadillo Teguise [1]** takes place every Sunday from 10.00 - 14.00 o'clock in the former island capital Teguise. The village, sleepy on weekdays, turns into a huge market with over 500 stalls on Sundays. It is the absolute highlight on the island. From 11.00 a.m. onwards, the crowds of people push their way along the stands, as the choice is huge. From plagiarism, beautiful souvenirs and handicrafts you will see everything your heart desires.
On the square in front of the church Iglesia Nuestra Señora de Guadalupe, a folklore group performs dances in traditional costume to self-played music at around 11.30 am. The church is open and can be visited. In Calle Rayo, decorated with colourful flags, you will meet the artisans.
⓵ Arrival and departure to the market: You can travel to the market by rental car, public transport, taxi or organised trips. Guarded, paid parking spaces are available for motorists on the main road. Travelling by public transport or by taxi is no problem, but the return journey could be longer due to the masses of people.
Organized bus trips to the market are an advantage, as they offer a guaranteed seat in the bus.
Tip for car drivers: At the Campo de Fútbol Los Molinos, that is already recognizable from a distance through high metal posts, there are free parking places. Calle Gadifer de la Salle- 35530 Teguise

16.2 Handicraft market in Haría

Every Saturday, the **Mercado de Artesanía [2] is held** in the village square in front of the church from 10.00 to 14.30 hours.

The market was created in 2001 to promote the sale of artisan, regional and ecological products and to offer visitors a wide choice.

At the meanwhile up to 70 different stands, you can stroll past and shop in peace.

With the multitude of products it should not be difficult to find the right present.

TIP: Combine your Saturday excursion to the market with a visit to the Museo de Arte Sacro, which is located next to the church.

The Casa/Mueso César Manrique, the last residence of the island artist, is signposted and within walking distance. On the same road, just after the estate, you can purchase unique basketwork from the last basket weaver on the island.

By the way: At the signposted cemetery Cementerio of Haría you will find the last resting place of César Manrique.

17   Gastronomy

The climate and geographical location of the island have determined the development of agriculture, which is not very varied and whose products, combined with those from the sea, have been the basis of the island's traditional cuisine.

Due to the tourism boom of the last decades, the variety of dishes has increased without losing the traditional cuisine.

The typical fishes of the island, dorado, sama and vieja are prepared in a variety of tasty variations. There is also goat and rabbit meat, served with cooked "papas arrugadas", the Canarian shriveled potatoes, with red and green mojo sauce.

The typical dishes of the island are stews - "potajes", stockfish "Sancocho" and "Ropa vieja"- a stew of meat, potatoes, vegetables and chickpeas.

The goat's cheese must also be mentioned, which is produced in many variations according to an old tradition. Finally, no good wine should be missing, which comes from the wine growing areas between Mozaga and La Geria.

Gofio", a roasted maize flour, as well as barley, millet and wheat have always been part of the staple diet of the Canarians. Gofio is nowadays used to bind stews and to make desserts.

17.1 Products

Lanzarote produces a relatively large variety of products despite the lack of water, heat and winds laden with Sahara sand. Currently, fruit and vegetables such as onions, tomatoes, potatoes, sweet potatoes, watermelons and pumpkins are grown on an area of approximately 7,000 hectares.

Together with Fuerteventura, the island was long known as the granary of the Canary Islands, as in the centre of the island, cereals and corn were cultivated on the sandy fields.

Livestock breeding is mainly limited to goats, sheep and cows. The goat stands out here because it is also bred for milk production to make goat's cheese. The cheese is rich in proteins, calcium, phosphorus and vitamins A, B and D. About five litres of milk are needed to produce one kilo.

17.2 Fisheries

In the past, the island's fishing fleet was the most important in the Canary Islands, with bases in Arrecife, La Graciosa, Puerto del Carmen and Playa Blanca. With fishing rods and nets, fish such as tuna, pike, mackerel, grouper, hake and wreckfish were caught. Up to the 20th century, the most common way of processing fish in the island was to put it in salt, so that Lanzarote could additionally profit from this way of processing due to the countless salt works of that time.

17.3 Traditional dishes

The Canarian cuisine is Mediterranean. The most important meal is lunch. There are many possibilities for this and specially in Lanzarote, there are still traditional dishes offered as it has always been eaten in the island. You will soon notice the important relationship with the sea: fish soup, stockfish, fish with onions... The stockfish "Sancocho" is one of the most important dishes of the Canary Islands and is usually served with moss sauces and gofio.

The meat dishes come from the Canary Islands' livestock breeding. You can find goat meat and rabbit in different sauces. Broths and stews are also among the classic traditional dishes.

Unfortunately, there is no typical liqueur as it is known from the other islands. The Lanzaroteños brew their own liqueurs at home, or use well-known brands from the neighbouring islands.

18   Tapas- the little delicacies

Originally, the term tapas was derived from the Spanish word "tapar", which means to cover. In bars, small morsels were placed on the beer or wine glasses to protect the drinks from flies.

If one speaks of tapas in the meantime, this refers exclusively to the portion size. Tapas can generally be served with all kinds of food, be it olives, cheese, meatballs, potatoes, chickpeas, fish or meat. In Spanish, the tapas names sound much more melodious when speaking of aceitunas, queso, albondigas, papas arrugadas, garbanzas, pescado or carne.

For this reason, in local restaurants, if a menu is available, you will find the reference to tapas, a small portion, a "½ Racion" - half a portion, or a whole portion, a "Racion".

18.1 Restaurant recommendation Casa Félix

The rustic furnished **restaurant [3]** exists since 1987 and has a small terrace with sea view to the beach Playa Bastian. Here you should definitely take a look at the tapas menu translated into German. We offer papas arrugadas - potatoes Canarian style, fried sweet potatoes, small peppers, fried anchovies, fried fish and chicken sticks, fish and chicken croquettes, chickpea stew with meat, fish salad, fried sardine fillets, marinated tuna, fried moray eel, fried squid with green mojo sauce, breaded cheese with fig jam, dwarf squid, tortilla española, goulash, chicken thighs, pork, meatballs, Russian salad and dates in bacon coat TIP: Order a selection of the delicious **tapas [4]**, which are served on a large platter with Canarian sauces.

❶Daily 12- 22.30, ⌂ Calle La Rosa, 2- 35508 Costa Teguise

18.2 Restaurant recommendation Bar Stop

Authentic local cuisine can be sampled in the small **restaurant [5]** Bar Stop with only 5 tables. With daily changing dishes, no frills and no menu, you can choose the daily changing dishes at a counter.

❶The staff speaks some English. All you have to do is point to what you want to eat and say "tapas". All meals are freshly prepared daily and depending on demand the large bowls at the counter are empty. Tip: To get a seat and see the complete selection of **local cuisine [6]**, you should visit the restaurant at 13.00 hrs.

❶1pm to clearance sale, Plaza Nuestra Señora de los Remedios, 6- 35570 Yaiza

19   Gastronomy Events

At 2 annual events you will find the largest tapas selection on the island. On 30 May the autonomy of the Canary Islands, which was achieved in 1982, is celebrated in the capital **Arrecife [7].** Join the hustle and bustle with live bands and countless tapas stands offering delicious tapas for only 1€.☉ 12-00, Parque José Ramirez Cerda, 35500 Arrecife

At the end of November the huge gastronomic festival takes place in **Teguise [8].** Tapas and wines are offered for tasting at well over 100 stands. There is a colourful hustle and bustle and the masses push past the stands.

In order to taste tapas or wines you will have to buy tickets at stands with the sign "Venta de Bebidas y Tickets"- sale of drinks and tickets.

❶The tapas offer of the neighbouring islands might also be interesting. If you are on the island at the end of September, ask for the date of the event at the tourist information offices or at the hotel. On Sundays you can combine the Tapas Festival in Teguise with a visit to the market.

20   Museums

20.1 Tanit Museum - Museo Tanit

The **Tanit** Ethnographic **Museum [1]** is located in the centre of San Bartolomé, signposted.

It is family-owned and located in former wine cellars of a traditional Canarian house from 1735.

The founders of the museum, Mr. José Ferrer Perdomo and Mrs. Remy de Quintana Reyes, have been collecting all kinds of objects and information for countless years, in order to preserve Lanzarote customs and traditions, starting from their ancestors, the Majos, until today for posterity.

In the entrance area a folder with all information about the museum is handed out.

Family heirlooms from the last century and, in the meantime, almost daily **objects [2]** were collected, sorted and exhibited according to themes.

These include, among others: A music corner, millstones, stone mortars, volcanic stone basins, bars, an art gallery, a wine cellar used since 1780, camel baskets, threshing boards, a typewriter, winepresses, paintings, a Canarian still, Bookcases with brochures dating from 1912, the patron saint "Virgen de los Dolores" of the

island, ceramics, ethnography, a stone cheese mould, rushes, a bridal couple from Mojon in traditional dress, a water depot, a threshing floor, a Canarian wine cellar and the garden. In the courtyard there is a small chapel dedicated to "Nuestra Señora de Pino".
The museum is self-financed and is not supported by the island government. The proceeds from the entrance fees will be used to expand and maintain the property. The founder comes to the museum almost daily to expand the collection.
☻Mon-Sat 10-14, ♦children under 12 years free, ⌂ Calle Constitución, 1- 35550 San Bartolomé

20.2 House of Timple- Casa Museo Del Timple

In the centre of the former island capital Teguise, the **Casa Del Timple** is located diagonally opposite the church **[3]**.
It is a palace built in the 18th century, which has been converted into a museum. In three rooms a collection of more than 60 timbres was compiled. Timples are small 5-sided musical instruments, comparable to guitars on which traditional Canarian music was played and is still played at small concerts.

☻Daily 10-14, ♦3€, children under 12 years free, ⌂ Calle José Betancort,6- 35530 Teguise

20.3 Museum of Sacred Art in Haría- Museo de Arte Sacro

Through a wide avenue of laurel trees you head straight towards the church. From the outside, it appears simple, like almost all churches on the island. As one actually assumes an old masonry, it is astonishing that by entering it, the interior does not fit in any way to the old sacral building method. The question arises as to why there is a church in this old village with the architectural style from the 1960s. The explanation can be found in the **Museo de Arte Sacro [4]**, which is located to the right of the church in an old manor house.
Old photos in the exhibition rooms show what had happened: The old church Iglesia de Nuestra Señora de la Encarnación was destroyed by a heavy storm in 1956. Pictures in the first exhibition room document the fatal destruction. In the other rooms old relics are exhibited.
TIP: Combine your visit to the museum on Saturdays with the arts and crafts market on Saturdays.

☽Tue, Thu, Fri + Sat 10-15, free, 🦡☖Plaza Leon y Catillo,14- 35520 Haría

20.4 Open-air museum El Patio- Museo Agrícultural El Patio

The agricultural museum **El Patio [5]** is located at the LZ-20 in Tiagua. Dr. José Maria Barrete Fee (1924- 1993) founded the museum to preserve the ethnographic and cultural values of Lanzarote. The large facility consists essentially of 2 complexes. The former manor house from 1845 houses the ethnological museum. Among the topics described in German are National geography, thought-provoking texts, geology, pottery, architecture, folklore, traditional clothing, crafts and tourism. You will encounter old photographs, an exhibition of lava stones, pottery and chimney types.

At that time, the complex was the largest agricultural enterprise on the island, with 20 farmers working in agriculture with more than 15 camels. Interesting is the small house with patio, kitchen, bathroom, living room and bedroom, where the foreman of the estate lived until 1949. In the bedroom there are camp beds with straw mattresses. The carpets are made of woven palm branches.

The tour continues to a wine press, a bodega, a small cactus garden and a chapel.

Through the garden with plants typical of the island you will reach an animal enclosure with a camel, goats and chickens. Next to it is a windmill. This is followed by a second ethnological exhibition with pictures, ceramics, basketry, camel seats, carts, handicraft tools and everything that was needed for agriculture at that time. The bodega offers white and red house wine, as well as Moscatel for tasting.

Visit the beautiful, well-kept complex, with a farmhouse atmosphere, where you are taken back to the last century. From the upper cultivated fields you look over Famara to the island of La Graciosa.

☽Mon-Fri 10-17, Sat 10-14.30,🦡 6,50€, ☖Calle Echeyde,18- 35558 Tiagua

20.5 Molino de Tiagua

Not far from the El Patio open-air museum is the **Tiagua mill [6]**. It dates from the 19th century and is one of the best preserved mills on the island. The farming families from the village and the surrounding towns of La Vegueta, Tinajo, Tao, Soo and Muñique brought their grain and roasted corn kernels to the mill to be ground into flour or gofio. Thanks to extensive restoration work by the island government, the mill shines like in old times. Don't miss the inspection of the mill and the view of the old wooden mill.

☉irregular > Google, 🍴free, ⌂ **Avenida** Armiche,2- 35558 Tigagua

20.6 Aviation Museum- Museo Aeropuerto

The **Aviation Museum [7] is** located directly at the airport.

The airport building was used from 1946 to 1970. At that time, it was the highlight of the island, but it was no longer able to cope with the tourist rush of the 1970s, so that the current airport was built. It is impressive how small the beginnings were in Lanzarote. On request, the museum staff will guide you through the premises with additional explanatory descriptions.

In the first room there is a large picture with a 1930s shot of the Graf Zeppelin over Las Palmas in Gran Canaria.

Further photographs show the beginnings of aviation and a landing in the bay of Arrecife in 1924.

In the adjoining room is the former waiting room.

On the right side hangs a reproduction of the long mural that César Manrique designed for the airport in 1953. It presents the island from north to south and contains many recognizable motifs such as the Famara rock, the volcano la Corona, the wine region La Geria, typical houses, camels and the fire mountains up to Playa Blanca. The original is currently owned by the Fundación César Manrique. The purchase of the painting was documented on a sheet of paper which is in the typewriter on display. In 1953 the cost of the mural amounted to 10,817.00 pesetas.To the left of it, in the small room that is currently used for film screenings, there was the souvenir shop.

In the back area, on the right side, there was the ticket counter, a small bar and the localities.

A large photo behind the bar, in which the original floor is still preserved, makes the **VIPs of that era [8]** come alive. From right to left you will meet Camilo Pajuelo Arteaga, then head of the Civil Guard, Thomás Lamamié de Clairc, delegate of the Iberia Airlines, Antonio Diaz Carrasco, airport chief and Benjamin Madero, chief of the Arrecife battalion.

On the left side of the bar the passengers went to the exit. Before departure, they had to stand individually with their luggage on the large scale to determine the weight for the aircraft.

On the left side was the office of the airport director, where today is a small library with additional information about aviation.

In the front part of the building a narrow staircase leads to the upper floor to the control tower. Only a radio, a telephone, a watch, a pen and a book were enough to coordinate the flights. Frontal view of Terminal 2 of the current airport.

🕐 Mon-Sat 10-14h, 🎫free, ⌂ LZ-2>Aeropuerto> follow the MUSEO signs

20.7 Wine museum El Grifo- Museo El Grifo

The museum **EL Grifo [1] is** located in the wine-growing region of La Gería in the southwest of the island. On the country road LZ-30, which leads through the whole area, one bodega follows the other.

El Grifo is the oldest winery in the Canary Islands and one of the ten oldest in Spain. For more than 2 centuries it was owned by two families, of which the present owner family owned it for more than 5 generations. The museum is located in the old wine cellar, where there are historical devices for wine production from the 19th and early 20th century.

4 different grape varieties are grown, which are harvested between June and September, as follows Malvasia, Listan negro, Syrah and Moscatel.

At the entrance, after payment, a map is handed out, which leads through the museum's premises. Among others, the following exhibits will be on display:

One lever and beam press, one wine press, different presses, the wine label designed by César Manrique for his favourite wine, semidulce, a **cask maker [2]**, a wine press, a library and a laboratory.

The second building houses a large label exhibition. Next to the exhibition room is the manor house, which is not open to the public. In the rear part of the complex there is a vineyard with the peculiarity that the vines were planted in solidified lava hollows.

A small cactus garden forms the conclusion. After the tour there is the possibility of a wine tasting included in the entrance fee.

🕐Daily 10.30- 18h, 🎫entrance fee - 30 min. 7€, with guided tour - 40 min. 12€, with winery tour - 90 min. 15€, ⌂ El Grifo, LZ-30

20.8 Museum of History Arrecife- Museo de Historia

The museum **Museo de Historia de Arrecife [3]** is located in the **Castillo San Gabriel [4]** on the small island Islote de Fermina. It is located near the main shopping street Calle Castillo y Léon of Arrecife.

The castle can be reached by two bridges, the left one is called Puente de las Bolas and is a small drawbridge with two cannonballs on the pillars.

In the 16th century the castle was replaced by a stone fortress, which served to protect the port and the town.

A museum guide is handed out at the entrance with explanations to the overview boards.

TIP: Enjoy the unique view over the sea and the capital from the upper floor.

◍Mon-Fri 10-17, Sat 10- 14 hrs, ▮free, ⌂Calle Punta de la Lagarata- 35500 Arrecife

20.9 Cochenille Museum/ Museo de La Cochinilla

The **Museum Museo de la Cochinilla [5]** is located near the cactus garden on the main road that runs through Mala.

Already at the entrance cacti were planted, which are covered with cochineal grooves **[6]**.

The cochineal is a scale insect that was used for the production of natural red colours in the 19th century. For this purpose cacti were infected with the pest. However, the cultivation lost importance when the product could be chemically produced. In the meantime, the Cochinelle is experiencing a revival, so that old cactus plantations in Guatiza and Mala are being reforested and repaired.

The museum shows in detail the process of making cochineal, from planting and harvesting to the production of the final product. In the following shop you can also try and buy the new Aloe Vera liqueur, besides many Aloe Vera products.

◍Daily 10:30- 18, ▮free, LZ-42, ⌂Calle Villa Nueva,42- 35543 Mala.

20.10 Milana Association

In the premises of the former primary school of Mala is the founded association **Asociación Milana [7]**. In the foreground is the application of the natural cochineal dye. Worth seeing are the elaborately dyed handicrafts that are offered at the Saturday market in Haría. In small workshops you can paint pictures with the cochineal paint on Mondays from 9-11 am and decorate silk scarves from 11-13 pm.

◍ Mon-Fri 8-14, workshops Mon 9-13, ▮free, contribution to the cost of material at the workshop, ⌂LZ-42- km 5, main road through Mala, Calle Villa Nueva,10- 355543 Mala

① The handmade products are marked with the "Milana" sticker. When you buy, you support the local trade, handicrafts and contribute to the revival of cochineal breeding in the region.

21   Aloe vera

Aloe Vera is an ancient medicinal plant known for its healing properties and is used in cosmetic and pharmaceutical products.
The largest **Aloe Vera Museum [8]** is located in Punta Mujeres. It offers information boards about the history of the Aloe Vera plant, its cultivation and use. In two further niches one learns more about the salt production in Lanzarote and the former scale insect breeding.
Friendly employees provide detailed information about the products and application areas.
① Product information is available at: www.aloepluslanzarote.com
LZ-1> direction Jameos del Agua,Carretera Jameos del Agua- 35542 Punta Mujeres

22   Unique island artists

22.1 The last basket weaver of Haría

Shortly after the Casa/ Museo César Manrique in Haría you will find the last **basketry [1]** of the island on the right-hand side.
Señor Eulogio Concepcíon Perdomo [2] sits on a small, low chair in a garage with green doors and wicker baskets hung in front of them, and weaves baskets of various sizes. To do this, the 87-year-old cuts dried palm branches into thin long strips to weave them in the traditional way.
In the past, his work was more in demand, so he appeared in person at craft markets. In the meantime, due to his advanced age, sales are only held in his workshop. According to his own statement he needs half a day to weave a small basket. The processed palm branches are provided by the gardeners of the Casa/ Museo César Manrique.◉ Daily variable, ⌂**Calle** Elvira Sanchez- 35520 Haría
In 2019, in honour of the last basket weaver, was placed between 2 palm trees. ⌂ Calle La Longuera, in front of the signposted Taller Municipal de Artesanía

22.2 Autentica Ceramica Canaria

You will find traditional clay works, which were already made by the indigenous people of the Canary Islands, in the Atelier Ceramica in the Monumento al Campesino.

The artist first moved from his small studio in Maguez, which could have been described as a garage, to Haría and now works in the Monumento al Campesino.

Señor Joachim Reyes Betancort [3] makes the sound himself. For this purpose he mixes **volcanic earth with clay [4]**, kneading the mixture with his feet until a sufficient consistency is reached. When shaping his creations, he squeezes out the remaining small stones to obtain a smooth surface.

The finished objects are dried for several days and then fired by him in the public kiln in the village. The actual burning process takes two days. On the first day he lights a small fire and adds wood every two hours. The next day more wood is added. In the last 5 hours of the firing process the wood supply is increased again and the kiln is closed. It takes three to five days until the work has cooled down and can be removed.

By the way: All clay works are made without a potter's wheel.◉ Mon-Sat 10-17.45, ⌂ signposted, junction LZ-20+ LZ-30- 35559 Mozaga

22.3 The Jolateros - boats made of recycled tin

The Jolateros are located on the main road Carretera Los Castillos, shortly after the Castillo San José towards Arrecife- El Charco de San Ginés. On the right side of the road you can see a big windmill, on the left side there are small colourful little boats on black lava stones. From here you follow the **promenade [1]**.

A few steps further on you will also come across the open-air workshop.

The history of the **Jolateros [2]**, the only and last Lanzarote boatbuilders to make one-man boats from scrap metal, goes back to the 1930s. At that time, fishermen used to take these small boats to their cutters, nowadays they are only used for summer races for children in the Charco San Ginés in Arrecife.

Señor Antonio presents the production of his boats in miniature form to his visitors full of joy and passion. With scissors he cuts a strip from a tin olive oil can, takes a pair of pliers, bends the sharp edges inwards and then knocks them flat on a wooden board. Then he forms the boat's shape with his thumb and fingers, takes a glue, which he spreads on two small pieces of wood and pins them to the ends of the boat to fix them in place. To test the final seaworthiness of the small new work of art, he places it in a plastic bowl filled with water. The souvenir is ready for sale with an individual painting.

This old Lanzarote boat building art is worth seeing. Here you can buy a special kind of souvenir. The small boats can also be purchased as key rings for a small price.

By the way: According to the current state of affairs, it is not certain whether Señor Antonio will be allowed to remain at this location permanently, as the current owner would like to put the property to another use. Currently, if you don't see the metal boats and don't meet him, he is exhibiting his exhibits in the back of the Charco de San Ginés.

22.4 Studio Luciano Martín

The 66-year-old **painter Luciano Martín [7]** comes from Playa Blanca and studied at the University of Tenerife. Already at the age of 26 he exhibited his works in Düsseldorf, Cologne and Dortmund. He is enthusiastic about Germany, speaks good German and is the proud father of 3 children, 8 grandchildren and now 1 great-grandchild. In his **exhibition [8]** the paintings made of lava- olive stone and oil paint are particularly noteworthy.

🕐Daily 10-19 o'clock, 🌢free, ❶after purchase the dispatch takes place via Fed Ex, ⌂ Calle Roque Bentaiga, 35570 Femes- district Las Casitas

22.5 Studio Stefan Schultz

The German **potter Stefan Schultz [1]** has lived in Teseguite with his wife Anneliese Guttenberger since 1987. In an old farmhouse they exhibit their work for sale. In addition to glazed ceramics, he produces black ceramics fired in a wood fire, for which he draws his inspiration from historical sources and study trips. After a 7-week stay in Tibet in 2019, his latest creations are shaped by these impressions. His wife devotes herself exclusively to painting and printmaking.
🕐Mon-Fri 11-17, ⌂ LZ-404- Avenida Acorán 43-45, 35539 Teseguite **[2]**

22.6 Potter Birgit Groth

The German **artist Birgit Groth [3]** has lived on the island since 2007 and creates new individual works every day, which she lovingly implements. The clay and over 100 glazes are shipped from Germany and fired on the island in the neighbouring village of Mozaga.

Especially popular are her mouse cups, which are food-safe and, like all her creations, can be used for everyday use.

A special place among her works are the worrystones, for which there is the following story by the artist: "At that time there was a country in fantasies, where actually everything was normal. The weather was changeable, the people had work, the children raved like all children - so, a really normal country. Sure, sometimes it rained at the wrong time or the fish did not bite properly or the children did not obey.

But in one thing the people of this country were different from other people. No one complained, complained or lamented. And if one of them said something, then another one replied: "Tell that to your worry stone".

Yes, they were quite happy people - not that they didn't have problems, but one thing made them different from other people. Everybody had their own worry stone - and that's how it came about:

In former times people were full of worries and problems and everybody told them to everybody who also had worries again and there were more frequent replies and also arguments. One felt overburdened to listen to the problems of others even to one's own worries. People were often discontented and in a bad mood.

One fine day, a fisherman, filled with worry and anger, goes down to the beach. He collects a handful of stones and throws them out into the sea as far as he can. But a short time later the waves throw them back onto the beach and they trundle in front of his feet. Still angry he lifts the first of the rolling back stones and with a sweeping movement he wants to throw it back into the sea. But then he suddenly hears a voice: "Stop, you won't get anywhere like that".

Astonished, the fisherman takes his arm down and notices that the stone in his hand is speaking these words. With eyes wide open he stares at the stone. "I am sorry for you," says the stone and looks at the man, "and therefore I will help you and the people in your land.

He smiles a little "I'm a worrywart. You can entrust with all your needs and problems. I won't tell! You can tell me anything - I won't contradict you! All your troubles will remain closed within me - I will be silent."

Then the stone rolls his little forehead in folds and whispers so quietly that our fisherman has to hold the stone to his ear to understand even the last words. "I have told you everything now and I will never speak again. Believe me, your worries will not necessarily be reduced by me, but you now have me to talk and think about it in peace. Take all the stones around you and give them to the people in your land. You will feel better then". No sooner said than done. And after a short time, people became happier and more cheerful and if someone was grieving, then it was: Tell that to your worry stone?

Further exhibits can be found at: www.toepferei-lanzarote.de By the way: The artist also makes creations on customer request.

☉ Th+Fr 11- 13/ 15- 6pm, ⌂ Calle Los Morros,15-35542 Arrieta

22.7 Artesanía ES

The German **artist Sandra Eisen [4] is** dedicated to painting. In her abstract paintings she tries to express her personal relationship to Lanzarote. The use of iron paint, which oxidizes on the canvas and continuously changes its appearance, is to be emphasized.

☉ n. Association. +34 682340482/ sandra@buenavista-lanzarote.com, ⌂ Calle las Pardelas 10a, 35539 Nazareth

22.8 Casa Don Pillimpo- Teguise

You will find an imaginative, extraordinary **park of figures [5]** along the main street of Teguise. The exceptional artist José García Martín created white, larger-than-life figures and incomparable curiosities in his front garden. In a conversation he said: "I have worked in the fields all my life, I am now retired and pray daily. With a moped he drove through the community with his life-size plastic barbie figure, which he had tied around sheets of music. Pillimpo was so appreciated and popular that no one was angry with him. Nevertheless, he grumbled: " Here there is no culture, no Bohemia and absolutely nothing."

① The exceptional artist José García Martín died in May 2019 at the age of 86. You can still benefit from his work. It is uncertain whether the heirs will sell the property and the figures will no longer be seen.

22.9 Taller Municipal de Artesanía

Not far from the centre of Haría, you will find the Taller Municipal de Artesanía artists' house, which is signposted. On 2 floors you can watch the artists in the process of creating their works. On the ground floor leather goods are produced at Mayeh- Artesanos. Miguel Clavijo makes pottery in the old canarian style. The jeweller Mario Francechin creates individual silver and gold jewellery with lava stones. On the upper floor, the **painter Itziar Alvarez [6] draws** inspiration for her works on canvas and wood from the island landscape. A colourful mixture of different handicrafts such as wickerwork, embroidery and clay pots completes the offer.

☺Ceramics Mon- Fr 9-14, painting Tue- Fr 9-15, jeweller Mon- Fr 9-14, leather Mon- Fr 8-14.30, ⌂ Calle la Longuera, 35520 Haría

➊On Saturdays you can find all the artists at the handicraft market Mercado Artesanal in Haría from 10-14.30 hours. Tip: Worth visiting is the adjacent market Mercado Municipal de Abastos. Organic products, fresh cakes and pastries, fish, meat, fruit and vegetables are offered. The tapas bar with local cuisine is a popular meeting point for islanders and police officers of the local Policia Municipal, who stop here for lunch.

☺ Biotienda organic food shop Mon-Sat 9-15, Dulceria confectionery Mon-Sat 10-16, Pescados y Mariscos fish shop Thu-Sat 9-14, Carnes Frescas meat products Thu-Sat 9-14, Frutas y Verduras fruit and vegetables Mon-Sat 9-14. The tapas bar is open from Monday to Saturday from 9-16.

22.10 Exposición de Arte- El Aljibe art exhibition

Directly in front of the Ayuntamiento de Haría town hall is the small square **Plaza de Constitución [7]**, under which changing art exhibitions are located. The name "El Aljibe" translates as water cistern. In Lanzarote, water has always been a scarce commodity, as neither ground water nor springs exist. In 1937, the wealthy merchant Emilio Rodríguez was asked by the municipality to build a water cistern for the poor population of the village of Haría. In 2000 the Aljibe no longer played a role on the island due to the good water supply and was converted into an exhibition hall. After the modification of the old "water tank", the 200 sqm showroom shines in a new light.

☺ Mon-Fri 9-13, 17-19, Sat 9-19, Sun 10-16,♨ free, ⌂ Plaza de la Constitución,1 -35520 Haria

22.11 Centro de Artesanía- Yaiza

The **arts and crafts centre [8]** is located on the way to the Fire Mountains in the south of the island. Beside a café, souvenir shops and manufactured clothes in the African look, the studio Sandra is to be emphasized. The artist creates individual jewellery from dried pansies.

☺ Mon-Fri 10am-6pm, Sat 10am-5pm, ⌂ Calle Vista de Yaiza,32-35570 Yaiza

23   Selected discovery tours

23.1 *Fascinating viewpoints*

On Lanzarote there are unique viewpoints from which you can enjoy fantastic views and take beautiful photos when the weather is clear.

Mirador del Rio [1]: From the café and the observation deck you can see the island of La Graciosa.

In Guinate, at the end of the village, you can once again enjoy the view of La Graciosa free of charge. The pretty **tile [2]** on the wall with the inscription "Dejate Llevar" means "Let yourself be carried along". ⌂ LZ-201>Guinate- Calle La Majadita- 35541 Guinate

Gran Hotel Arrecife City: On the 17th floor of the Grand Hotel there is a public café, with **views over Arrecife [3]**, up to Puerto del Carmen and Fuerteventura. ⌂ Calle Islas Canarias- 35500 Arrecife

The church **Ermita de Las Nieves [4]**: Unique panorama over the whole island to Fuerteventura. ⌂ LZ-10>signposted Las Nieves> Calle Gadifer de la Salle- 35539 Teguise

Pirate Museum- **Museo de la Pirateria [5]** in Teguise: Magnificent view over Teguise and the whole island to Fuerteventura. ⌂ Castillo de Santa Bárbara- 35530 Teguise

Femés [6]: When the weather is clear, you can see from the panoramic terrace on Playa Blanca to the white beaches of Corralejo on Fuerteventura, with the island of Los Lobos in front of it. For photos like in the Caribbean, you should translate to La Graciosa. LZ-702, Plaza de San Marcial- 35570 Femés

Antigua Rofera lava flow **[7]**: The bizarre lava formations in Teguise are suitabl e as a backdrop for unforgettable photos.
LZ-1> LZ-1A> LZ-404

By the way: unfortunately, in Lanzarote one can never say when it is the best time to make some nice pictures. Spring and autumn are, from experience, the best seasons to take pictures of viewpoints. However, the weather situation can be volatile even during these months. Strong winds can occur all year round and after a few hours the clouds can blow away, leaving a bright blue sky. But in Lanzarote, at "Calima", one speaks about a misty weather that brings dusty and sandy winds from Africa to the island. In the summer months it is mostly cloudy until midday and there is often a light drizzle, but it lasts only a short time. The landscape is accordingly kept in monotonous brown tones. After lush but short rains in the late autumn months, Lanzarote shines in a lush green with flowers.

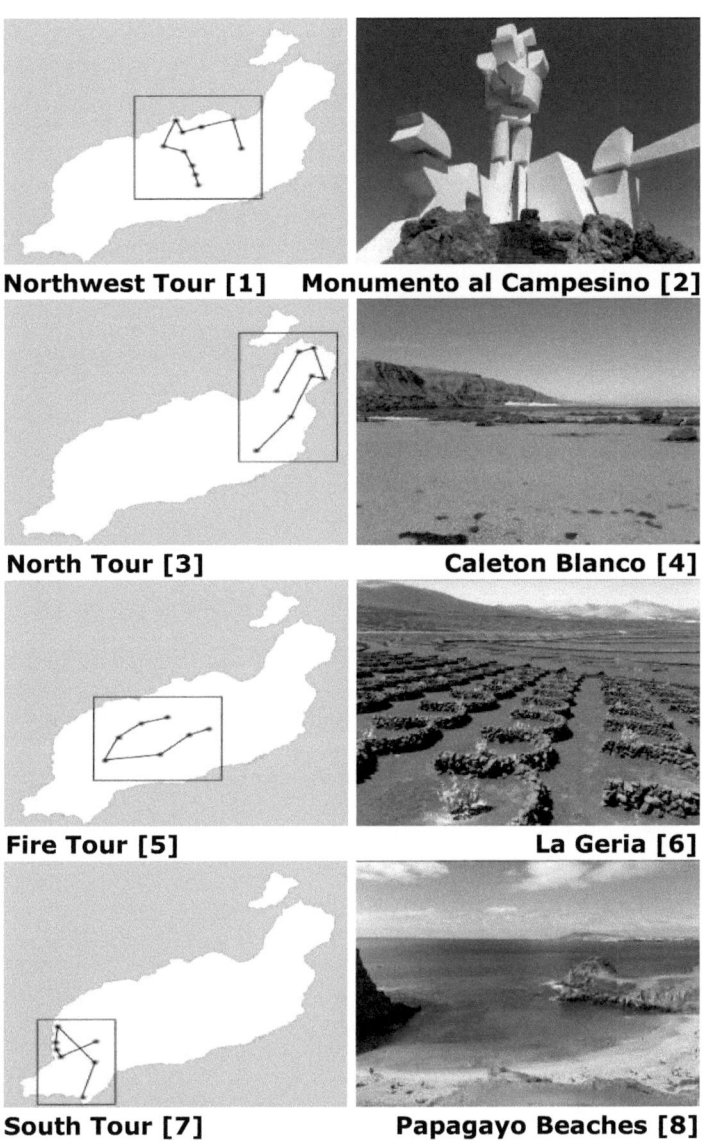

Northwest Tour [1]   **Monumento al Campesino [2]**

North Tour [3]   **Caleton Blanco [4]**

Fire Tour [5]   **La Geria [6]**

South Tour [7]   **Papagayo Beaches [8]**

23.2 The Northwest

The **northwest tour [1]** starts in the geographic center of the island in San Bartolomé at the **Monumento al Campesino [2]**.

You drive towards Tinajo through the villages of Mozaga, Tao and Tiagua. In Tiagua there is the possibility to visit the farm museum Museo Agricola El Patio.

From Tinajo we continue towards La Santa, where the sports and leisure club of the same name is located.

On the way back you will pass El Cuchillo and Soo until you reach Caleta de Famara, a fishing village where you can watch surfers on the beach and have a beautiful view of the island of La Graciosa.

Also head for the former island capital Teguise, which captivates with its picturesque old town and can look back on 500 years of history.

On the volcanic mountain above Teguise there is the Castillo Santa Barbara, from which you have a wonderful wide view over the whole island.

23.3 The contrasting north

The **north tour [3]** towards Órzola starts in the village of Tahiche, where the Fundación César Manrique, the famous house with the underground lava bubbles, is located. From here take the LZ-1 in the direction of Orzola. In Mala you can visit the new Cochenillen Museum. In Guatiza the cactus garden Jardín de Cactus can be visited.

Passing through the towns of Mala and Arrieta, the path leads towards Orzola- Jameos del Agua. Here you have the possibility to visit the Jameos del Agua, the cave with the small white albino crabs, as well as the Cuevas cueva, which is located a little further up.

On the continuation of the journey, we drive along the coast, through the Malpais de La Corona, the green heart of Lanzarote. The road passes beautiful bays, the last of which, **Caleton Blanco [4], is one of the** most beautiful on the island.

23.4 The volcanic fiery center

The **fire tour [5]** starts in the geographic center of the island in San Bartolomé, at the Monumento al Campesino, where the farm museum is located. From here we head towards Masdache, with destination **La Geria [6]**, the unique area characterized by its traditional wine growing.

The road ends in Uga, from where you drive towards Yaiza with the destination of the National Park Parque Nacional de Timanfaya.

Passing the camel resting place Echadero de Camellos with the possibility for a camel ride, the road leads directly to the national park.

Continuing towards Tinajo, you will find the Visitor Centre, the Centro de Visitantes, with audiovisual presentations and a footbridge that leads into the rugged volcanic landscape of the Timanfaya region.

From here you can reach Mancha Blanca with the Ermita de Los Dolores, the patron saint of the island. Finally, towards La Geria, at the end of the road that crosses the beautiful volcanic landscape, you can return north towards Monumento al Campesino, or south towards La Geria.

23.5 The south coast

South Tour [7]: You will take the southern highway LZ-2 towards Yaiza, through the village of the same name, which is characterized by its white and well-kept architecture. From here you will head for the unique coastal ensemble: The Salinas de Janubio, Los Hervideros, El Lago de los Clicos and the fishing village of El Golfo.

In the extreme south is Playa Blanca, with the famous **Papagayo beaches [8]**.

On the way back you will pass Femes to enjoy a beautiful view over the south of the island to Fuerteventura. On the continuation of the journey, we pass Las Casitas de Fémes and return to the main axis LZ- 2, which leads in all directions.

23.6 Hike Montaña Colorada

At the LZ-56 direction Timanfaya there are 2 **stone walls [1]** with the inscription Municipio de Tinajo on both sides after a short distance. Here you follow the road towards Timanfaya.

For orientation, the **Montaña Colorada [2]** is the second volcano on the right side of the road. At the roadside there is a small white and green sign with the inscription LZ- 56 KM 4, followed shortly after by a stationary radar, a bend and a no overtaking sign. Immediately after that you can turn right from the road onto an ash field and park.

Now the border can start, a nice walk of 45-minutes through an impressive landscape. The degree of difficulty is low, as the path runs almost level around the volcanic cone. At 15 points of interest there are boards that provide additional information in German.

After a short time you will discover why the volcano "Vulcano Colorado" = "colored volcano" carries its name: You will encounter a red-hot volcanic landscape, which you would not have expected on the previous page.

Here is a huge **monolith [3]**, which flew 20 km to this spot during the eruptions of the Timanfaya.
By the way: You will find the sparkling olive stones directly in the large field in front of the parking lot. It is not expressly forbidden to take stones with you, but you should leave it with smaller specimens and pack them in your suitcase and not in your hand luggage. ⌂ LZ-30, km15> LZ-56> after km 4 before the right turn

23.7 Hiking tour Montaña del Cuervo

The Montaña del Cuervo is located at the LZ- 56, direction Timanfaya National Park. After a short drive 2 **lava stone walls [1]** with the inscription Municipio de Tinajo follow. Shortly after that, on the right and left side, on smoothed out ash places, there are parking facilities. Now follow the trail, which is marked with stones at the edges.
The **path [4]** will be documented in German language after a 10-minute walk by the operators of the national park.
This is followed by a nice walk through a fascinating **landscape [5]** to the volcano and into the **crater [6]**.
Out of the crater, you can either turn right to go back to the parking lot or turn left to walk around the volcano.
The mini-hike takes about 1.5 hours, if you also walk around the volcano. Easy degree of difficulty, but you should wear closed shoes, as the path is partly rocky.
Tip: Combine this hike with the Montaña Colorada, which is within easy reach, almost opposite. ⌂ LZ-30, km15> LZ-56> between km 4 and 5

23.8 Volcano Monte Corona- View into the crater

To the north is the highest volcano, Monte Corona, at 609 m. Take a look into the **crater [7]** and take extraordinary photos. The way is not signposted. It starts in the small village of Ye and is located at LZ-10 between Guinate and the Mirador del Río, more precisely, between the church and the restaurant, right next to the house with the number 18.
The easiest way is to park in front of the small church and walk down the road towards Mirador del Río. After the first house on the right-hand side there is a large vineyard. The road gets a little wider on the right side, the road marking is dotted here. Now you see a yellow and white road sign with the inscription LZ-201 KM 4, behind it there

is a garbage container. Directly behind it on the right field, the **path** begins **[8]**.

It leads past semicircular stone walls, in which wine is planted in the middle, metal poles with empty plastic bottles hanging from their tips, overgrown stone walls, higher and higher up to the crater. The further up you get, the stonier the path becomes. The ascent takes about 30 minutes, the way back takes just as long.

For directional orientation you can hold on to the large palm tree. You will enjoy a wonderful view over the coast and in the distance you will see the Mirador del Río, which can be recognized by the queues of cars parked in front of it.

Recommendation: Make sure you wear sturdy shoes, as the path is very rocky in the upper part.

24   Cheese dairies- Queserías

In Lanzarote the cheese production has a long tradition. The handmade goat cheese can be bought in the local cheese dairies and at weekly markets.

24.1 Cheese dairy El Faro

The **Queseria El Faro [1] is** located in the north of the island, in the direction of Teguise, on the LZ-30, parallel to the main road, behind a high wall, you will discover the countless goats that provide the milk for the cheese.

The courtyard of the company is kept very simple and in the tiny shop there is a manageable cheese counter.

The products offered include fresh goat's cheese, young, medieval and mature goat's cheese, each in the varieties natural, paprika and gofio, and smoked goat's cheese.

In 2014, El Faro was awarded the gold medal for its smoked goat's cheese at the official Canary Islands cheese competition.

☉ Mon-Fri 8-15, Sat 8- 13h, ⌂ LZ-30, between km 8 and 9

24.2 Cheese Dairy Rubicón

The **Queseria Rubicón [2]** is located in Femés, in the south of the island. It is located below the small church of the village and is signposted at the roundabout.

On offer are fresh goat's cheese, matured, smoked goat's cheese, as well as cheese with oregano, gofio and paprika powder. Next to the cashier's counter there is a selection of cheeses that can be tasted.

❶The special feature of the Rubicon cheese dairy is that it is possible to have the cheese vacuum-packed so that it can be taken to Germany. Fresh goat's milk and goat's yoghurt are offered daily. By the way: Opposite the cheese dairy there is a volcanic mountain on which the farm's own goats run around.
❷Mon-Fri 10-19, Sat + Sun 10-15, ⌂ 35570 Femés

25   Bodega Los Almacenes/ Mama Trina

The **Bodega Los Almacenes [3]** is located on the LZ-1 in the direction of Mirador del Río, in the north of the island. A few bends after the strikingly large yellow house on the left, a path leads directly to Los Almacenes.

In the **sales room [4],** besides wine and liqueurs, the famous Mama Trina jams and mojo sauces are offered for tasting and sale. Almost all products are from our own production.

The "Mama Trina" products, made according to old family recipes, are also available in many supermarkets and at the weekly markets.

Tip: Especially the jams and mojo sauces are a great souvenir for those who stayed at home.❷ Daily 11am-6pm, ⌂ LZ-1

26   German Bakery Andy Bread- Panadería Andy Bread

The green entrance door leads directly into the bakery. It smells wonderfully delicious of fresh pastry, rolls and bread.   The special thing about the bread is that it is made from wholemeal flour without baking agents and contains neither enzymes nor additives. For **Andy bread [5]** the dough is prepared with a 4-step natural sourdough made from wholemeal rye flour. The natural sourdough is allowed to ferment for 48 hours in alternate cool (strong taste) and later warm surroundings (yeast formation). This makes it milder than doughs produced faster (some sourdoughs only have 3-5 hours time to mature) and much more tasty and digestible than "natural sourdoughs" made from artificial souring agents, the so-called "artificial sourdoughs". Then wholemeal flour, water and a little salt are added and the dough is prepared, which rests for several hours again. Since the foundation of the company in 2003, a residual quantity is taken as a basis for the next sourdough.

be offered: Wholegrain rye bread (oat flakes), wholegrain rye bread, wholegrain rye nut bread, wholegrain spelt bread (also with sunflower or pumpkin seeds), farmhouse bread (also with sunflower or pumpkin seeds), large rye nut bread, farmhouse bread, gluten-free bread, boxed white bread, white baguette, Grain baguette, surprise baguette, ciabatta, grain roll, wholemeal spelt roll, pretzel

roll, pretzel, croissant, chocolate croissant, ham cheese eye stick, raisin snail, raisin roll, muesli stick, yeast plait and cake in the varieties cherry, apple, plum, cheese and onion.
◑Fri+Sa 7-12 a.m., ⌂ Calle Gabriel Diaz, 9- 35572 Tias

27   Lanzarote Aquarium- Costa Teguise

The **aquarium [6] is** located in the Centro Comercial El Trébol in Costa Teguise.
Through the souvenir shop you go down into the underwater world with 33 aquariums with a total volume of 1000 cbm. The tour is divided into 3 themes: Canary coasts, tropical reefs and open sea. In the differently sized aquariums you can meet the following sea creatures: bream, sea urchins, large tiger fish, mussels, snails, starfish, koi, moray eels, crabs, sea urchins, lobsters, octopuses, rays, cat sharks, "Nemo", fish camouflaged in the sand, anemones, spiny fish and small sharks.
If you walk through the small tunnel of the aquarium, the sharks are within reach.
The environmental protection programme that the Aquarium supports in relation to the turtles is noteworthy: "...The Aquarium Lanzarote participates in the programme for the conservation and protection of the Caretta turtles, supported by the Municipal Environmental Protection Agency. The aim of the project is to preserve the species of these turtles, which are threatened with extinction. The turtles in the aquarium were found severely injured in the sea. After life-saving operations and healing of all injuries, these animals were admitted to our installations in order to provide them with a species-appropriate rehabilitation and then reintegrate them into their natural environment, the open sea. Only those animals that could not survive in the open sea due to serious injuries remain in the aquarium."
❶For aquarium fans and children worth seeing. In a maximum of 35 minutes the tour is finished and you are at the exit.
◑Daily 10-18 o'clock, ♨14 €, children 4-12 years. 9€, ⌂ Calle Las Acacias, 35508 Costa Teguise

28   Aquapark Costa Teguise

The **Aquapark [7]** is open from the beginning of April to mid-November and is already getting on in years. In the main season it is more than difficult to find a couch, at the slides you have to show stamina. They are no longer permitted above a body weight of 100 kg.

① From Costa Teguise it can be reached on foot or by taxi. A shuttle service to and from Puerto del Carmen and Playa Blanca is offered for a fee of 4€. More information at: www.aquaparklanzarote.es
☻ During the season daily 10-18 o'clock, ♨23,5€, children 4-12 years. 17€, from 15 o'clock 17€ and 13€ respectively, ⌂ Avenida el Golf,315- 35508 Costa Teguise

29   Aqualava Playa Blanca

The **Aqualava Water Park [8]** is open all year round. It has 5 water slides, a current canal, a wave pool, a children's play area and a restaurant where you can spend a nice day. The pools are heated with geothermal energy.
①In addition to day tickets, 1- and 2-week subscriptions are offered at a discount at the ticket office. More information is available at: www.aqualava.net
☻ Daily 10-17 o'clock, 21€♨, children 14,5€, Abo 1 Wo. 55 or 45€, Abo 2 Wo. 75 or 60€, ⌂ Calle Gran Canaria- 35580 Playa Blanca

30   Hop On Hop Off Arrecife

To get a small overview of the island capital Arrecife and the surrounding area, you can get on and **off the** train with the **Hop On Hop- Off [1]** principle as often as you like.
The company City Sightseeing Arrecife offers 2 tours with 16 stops that can be used in one day with the ticket. ① You can board and disembark as often as you like, the fare is due once at the start of the journey. You will receive a map of the city as well as headphones, which provide interesting and enlightening information about the sights of the tour during the tour. Included is the entrance to the Castillo San José and the Archaeological Museum, as well as a "gift" at the Marina Lanzarote and a tapa with drink at the Charco de San Gínes.
More at: www.city-ss.es/en/destination/arrecife/
☻Daily 10-16 o'clock, start: 10 o'clock in front of the Castillo San Gabriel at the junction to the main shopping street Castillo Leon y Castillo in Arrecife,
♨ 12€, children 7-12 years. 6€, 3-7 years. 4€.

31   Líneas Romero- Puerto del Carmen <> Puerto Calero

The company Líneas Romero offers a boat service with the **Express Waterbus [2]** between Puerto del Carmen and Puerto Calero and vice versa. You can sit on deck in the sun and enjoy the great view of the rugged lava coast of the island. During a short stopover the hatches of the boat are opened to view the underwater world off the coast.

In both harbours you can go ashore and explore the town or experience the extensive gastronomy. ➊ The tickets are available in the old port of Puerto del Carmen directly in the office of Lineas Romero or at the end of the port of Puerto Calero in the ticket shop. Unfortunately, the excursion is not recommended for people who get seasick quickly, as the ship wobbles slightly when leaving the ports. More at www.lineasromeros.com

☉Departure: <u>Puerto Calero> Puerto del Carmen</u> :10>11.15>12.45> 14.15>15.45, Departure: Puerto del Carmen> <u>Puerto Calero: 10.30></u> <u>12.00> 13.</u>30> 15.00> 16.30, one way 8€, children from 2-11 years 6€, return 12€ and 7€.

32   Pardelas Park- Pardelas Restaurant

The **Pardelas Park [3]** is a small petting zoo and is located in the north of Lanzarote.

At the cash desk you will get a filled plastic bucket **[4]** to feed the animals. You can see hares, chickens and roosters, peacocks, ducks and chicks, pot-bellied pigs, ponies, horses, donkeys and goats. It is fascinating how well all animals know the buckets. As soon as you put the bucket on the ground, the ducks help themselves. The horses and the donkey scratch their hooves. If you do not feed the goats immediately, they will jump at you.

There is a large playground with slides and swings in the complex. Children have the opportunity to ride a donkey and make pottery.➊ The Las Pardelas restaurant is part of the complex. Since 2012, Swiss chef Viktor Spillmann has been responsible for the Canarian cuisine. The park is especially suitable for parents with small children and business people who like animals.

☉Daily 10am-6pm, ⌂ LZ- 203> signage Granja Recereativa Zoo> Calle la Quemadita, 88- 35541Orzola

33   Rancho Texas Park

Rancho Texas Park in Puerto del Carmen is a combination of a zoo and a small water park with slides. Among the new attractions are **penguins [5]** and a **dolphin show [6]**. On the picturesque route through the park you can observe all the animals. At no time does the feeling arise that the animals are locked up. It should be emphasized that the Zoo has taken in animals from tortured captivity, which are cared for here and spend their retirement.

Adult white tigers and pumas, which were kept in small circus metal cages, have been given a large enclosure in the park. The penguins from the closed zoo in Guinate also visibly feel comfortable in the new installations of the facility.

There are 5 different shows in the park:

10.45> Parrots- 1st performance
11.30> Dolphins 1st performance
12.10> Lasso show- only performance
12.30> Sea lions- 1st performance
13.00>Eagle- 1st performance
13.30> Parrots- 2nd performance
13.45> Dolphins 2nd performance
14.30> Sea lions- 2nd performance
15.00> Eagle- 2nd performance
16.00> Parrots- 3rd performance

① The lasso show takes place in the huge fast food restaurant. Especially parents with children will get their money's worth. For the kids there are playgrounds, play areas, western carriages, pony rides and a large adventure pool in the water park. For further information please visit: www.ranchotexaslanzarote.com

①Shuttle bus in Puerto del Carmen free of charge. From Costa Teguise and Playa Blanca chargeable. ④ Daily 9.30- 17.30, 30€, children under 12 years 22€, LZ-40> signposted, Alcalde Cabrera Torres, 35510 Puerto del Carmen

34   Bodega La Querencia

The privately run bodega is located in the wine-growing area of La Geria.

The owner **Señor Luciano [7] is the** 5th generation of the family to cultivate wine. On 30,000 square meters they produce 7-8000 liters annually. At the back of the bodega there is a walled corner where the grapes are treaded with the feet and then put into the wine press. The juice is then pressed. Produced are Malvasia, Listán blanco and negro, and Moscatel.① You can taste the wines that are bottled and corked before your eyes when you buy them. ④ Mon-Sat 11am-6pm, ⌂ LZ-30, Carretera Uga, 35570 La Geria (Coming from San Bartolomé, La Querencia is the first winery on the left before the Bodega Rubicon. On the road signs with the inscription "Vino- Wine" indicate the access road).

35   Telamon- The Titanic of Las Caletas bay

On 21.10.1981 the Greek **cargo ship Telamon [8]** left San Pedro on the African Ivory Coast with course for the port of Thessaloniki. The freight consisted of logs and fuel. When almost 6 weeks later, on 31.10.1981, the ship was in the strait La Bocaina between Lanzarote and Fuerteventura, an enormous storm caused some extreme damages to the cargo space of the freighter that was then nearly 30 years old. The captain declared a state of emergency and the freighter was maneuvered to the shore of Las Caletas Bay so as not to block the port of Los Marmoles.

At the time, no further attention was paid to the construction logs, but 260 tons of heavy oil and 60 tons of diesel had to be pumped out carefully and carefully to prevent an oil catastrophe.

Since the Greek owner abandoned his cargo ship, another interested party decided against repair and removal due to the estimated costs of 100 million pesetas, today approx. 600,000 €, the Telamon remained there until today. During a later storm the freighter broke into 2 parts, so that only the part above the water surface can be seen.

Due to its size, the Telamon was the big attraction of Lanzaroteños, but it turned into a ruin that became dangerous for bathers and divers.

The president of the Chamber of Commerce, José Torres, was the first to sound the alarm and to point out the fatal condition of the freighter in a letter to the port authority. In 2009 the Telamon attracted media interest for the last time. It was the ship's cargo. The tree trunks, which had been lying on land for almost 30 years, exposed to the weather and only just escaped destruction by fire, were staged by the Spanish urban planner José Maria Pérez Sánchez as a large sculpture in the roundabout on Las Cucharas beach in Costa Teguise. After a storm in September 2016 the sculpture was removed without replacement. In addition, in the same month a diving and camping ban was imposed on the section around the Telamon, which is still in force today.

36   Anti-boredom activities

You are bored and have already visited everything worth seeing? Even if Lanzarote seems to be rather small, there are more possibilities than one would expect. Starting with water sports, safaris and hikes up to visits to the casino, there are countless alternatives to the pool. In order to get an overview of the entire programme, it is best to visit a tourist information office located in each holiday resort. All current flyers are available here and on request you will be informed about current festivals and events.

37   Lanzarote with children

Highly recommended:
- Hop- on Hop- Off Arrecife- Sightseeing with the magic train
- Rancho Texas Park- Animal shows and bathing fun
- Airport Museum- Nostalgia to touch
- Pardelas Park- Petting zoo and animal feeding
- Caleton Blanco- Sunbathing and swimming in a lagoon
- Water Parks- Costa Teguise and Playa Blanca
- Farming village in the Monumento al Campesino- Creative workshops
- Aquarium Costa Teguise- Fish world to look at
- Asociación Milana- Painting pictures with cochinelline colour

38   General Information Canary Islands

Pharmacies
- There are pharmacies in all larger towns. In contrast to other Countries, you can also get many medicines here without a prescription and much cheaper.

Bathing safety
- Every year people die while bathing in the Canary Islands! Please note that the Atlantic Ocean is extremely dangerous in the Canarian waters. Strong currents, undercurrents and suddenly appearing waves with strong suction effects are not uncommon. Even experienced professional swimmers have already lost their lives through carelessness. As soon as the red flag is raised, bathing is absolutely forbidden. Never go into the water just because a few people have already taken a bath. When the flag is yellow, it is already recommended to stay only in the area close to the beach. If you witness a swimming accident, do not swim after it under any circumstances. Inform the lifeguards at the guarded beaches if available, otherwise call 112. You can also report the incident in German.

Banks and money
- There are banks and ATMs in all larger towns. When withdrawing money with a cash card, however, there are sometimes high fees, as is the case everywhere abroad. It is

best to have a small supply of cash with you and pay all other amounts with a credit card.

Bus / public transport
- The public buses on the Canary Islands are called guaguas and run regularly between all the larger towns. You will find the departure times directly at the bus stops (Paradas). The bus tickets are quite cheap in the Canarian Islands.

Theft
- The quota of crimes is very low in the Canarian Islands, but of course there are also here "bad fingers". Therefore please do not leave anything of value open and visible. In case of theft or crime, you can call the police directly with 112. In order to be able to assert your claims with your insurance company in your Countrie, you must have a police protocol issued.

Shopping and business hours
- In the Canary Islands there are no fixed shop opening hours. In tourist areas, shops are often open continuously from morning to evening. These shops are also open on Sundays. In normal residential areas or big cities there is often the classic lunch break between 13-17 o'clock.

Festivals and public holidays
- In the Canary Islands many general and island-typical fiestas are celebrated. Individual communities on each island also have their local festivals and holidays. The Cannario likes to celebrate. In contrast to other Countries, holidays that fall on a weekend are celebrated on the following Monday. Depending on the island and municipality, it is recommended to google on the Internet beforehand. The festivals are often very interesting, as they are celebrated with original clothes and in a highly traditional way.

Photography
- There are no specific additional rules. However, as everywhere else in the world, you should not film or record the police or military areas. Otherwise it is called with pleasure when photographing "fire freely".

church services / masses
- The Canarian population is mostly catholic and there is an Ermita or church in almost every village. The opening hours are always posted at the church, but the Sunday service at noon is always obligatory. Since many architecturally interesting churches only open during trade fairs, a visit to a trade fair is definitely recommended.

Rental car
- In the Canarian Islands, it is already possible to get some rental cars for a reasonable price. There are rental stations in every port, at the airport and also in all tourist places. Reservations can also be made in advance via the Internet.

Emergencies
- The general emergency number is 112 without area code! You can also contact the ship's reception desk directly, they have numbers of doctors, embassies, etc.

Opening hours
- In the tourist areas, the shops are usually open 7 days a week from morning to evening. But in the Canarian Islands, there is still the classic siesta, so that the shops are closed from 13-17 o'clock. As there is no law on shop opening hours as in Germany, you will always find a place to shop and linger.

Sun
- Attention. The Canary Islands are not far from the equator, so that even in December and January UV values are reached that in Germany only occur in summer. Do not be fooled by the clouds in the sky. Depending on your skin type, it is therefore advisable to use sunscreen both when going ashore and on the ship.

39   Heads up! Bathing accidents

It is frightening that every year so many holidaymakers have to lose their lives in the Atlantic. Partly out of ignorance, but also arrogance, because they think they are good swimmers. The extreme undercurrents in this part of the Atlantic Ocean are underestimated, which will be the downfall of every professional swimmer. Only within a few seconds can a "funny" wave become a deadly threat. Even in absolute proximity to the beach, the sea can suddenly retreat and develop a suction effect that even a full-grown elephant could not withstand. Guarded beaches with lifeguards, who in case of emergency put themselves in absolute danger of their lives to save the bathers, are unavoidable. Tragically, countless first-aiders have also become victims of the Atlantic last year. On average, every week a person loses his life in the Canarian waters. According to the current statistics from 2019, this also includes 3 people whose bodies have not been located in the sea.

The total number of deaths by drowning in 2019 was 57:

Gran Canaria 20
Tenerife 14
Lanzarote 10
Fuerteventura 10
El Hierro 1
La Gomera 1
La Palma 1

By activity, 63% of drowned people were bathers, followed by fishermen, divers and water sports enthusiasts. 75% of the drowned are holidaymakers, 84% of them men and 16% women. They came from Germany, England, France, Italy, Norway, Sweden, Holland, Russia, Hungary, Poland and Switzerland.

40 Index

W

Water park Aqualava · 74

FSC
www.fsc.org
MIX
Papier aus ver-
antwortungsvollen
Quellen
Paper from
responsible sources
FSC® C105338